"*Do Greater Things* is filled with truth and carries power because of the way Robby actually lives out a supernatural lifestyle, walking in signs and wonders in everyday life. It is applicable to every believer, whether you feel called to ministry in the church or to part of a different sphere of influence. This is a must-read for anyone who wants to live a lifestyle like Jesus. I know you'll be transformed as you read it!"

Kris Vallotton, senior leader, Bethel Church, Redding, CA; co-founder, Bethel School of Supernatural Ministry

"Some people loom larger than life and others appear down-to-earth. My friend Robby Dawkins and his book *Do Greater Things* have the unique ability to do both, while inviting us into a life elevated. This book inspires you with stories, instructs you with Scripture and invites you into an authentic life of doing greater things."

Bob Hazlett, author, *God's Sound in a Raging World*; www.bobhazlett.org

"Robby Dawkins shares miracles God did through his own life as well as miraculous healings that occurred when other ordinary people stepped out in faith. Even great men and women of God struggle with fear, but Robby spurs us on to remember that Jesus said we will do greater things—and it's true!"

Heidi G. Baker, Ph.D., co-founder and CEO, Iris Global

"Robby Dawkins makes what seems complicated simple. His stories inspire you to get out and give it a try. His humility frees you to get back up and do it again. His boldness releases faith in you for miracles. His joy unlocks you for fun in the midst of the fight. Most of all, his witness invites you to live the greater things today!"

Danielle Strickland, author, speaker, advocate

"Robby Dawkins' faith, boldness and fearlessness function at such a high level that it is impossible for heaven not to respond. In *Do Greater Things*, Robby shares the secrets he has learned that have catapulted him to the level of spiritual authority he is currently walking in. We all need to read this book."

Brian "Head" Welch, co-founder, Korn;
New York Times bestselling author, *Save Me from Myself*

"Robby Dawkins' *Do Greater Things* invites the reader into a life of the supernatural. Robby is one of the bravest persons I know in the Kingdom of God—a powerful evangelist who thrives on the street. This book will show you how to better flow with the Holy Spirit. Anyone wanting to be encouraged to witness to the King and His Kingdom should buy and read *Do Greater Things*."

Randy Clark, D.Min., overseer, Apostolic Network
of Global Awakening; founder, Global Awakening

"There are certain individuals who with their life and boldness for God actually draw a line in the sand for every believer. I so appreciate the life of Robby, and his new book *Do Greater Things* provokes me not to settle for nominal living but rather to step into what Jesus instructed to anyone who follows Him. Be ready to be challenged and inspired to leave your comfort zone."

Eric Johnson, senior pastor, Bethel Redding

"Seventy years ago in 1947 a healing revival broke out with signs and wonders that had not been seen since Acts 2, when the age of the apostles exploded in the earth. Now once again that great wave is beginning to crest. Robby Dawkins has been a pioneer of this fresh wave—moving in words of knowledge and miraculous healings. This book will train, inspire and create faith so that you too can step into this great wave that will fill and heal the nations."

Lou Engle, co-founder, TheCall

DO GREATER THINGS

ACTIVATING THE KINGDOM
**TO HEAL THE SICK AND
LOVE THE LOST**

ROBBY DAWKINS

Chosen
a division of Baker Publishing Group
Minneapolis, Minnesota

© 2018 by Robby Dawkins

Published by Chosen Books
11400 Hampshire Avenue South
Bloomington, Minnesota 55438
www.chosenbooks.com

Chosen Books is a division of
Baker Publishing Group, Grand Rapids, Michigan

Printed in the United States of America

Library of Congress Control Number: 2017951673

ISBN 978-0-8007-9858-1

To protect the privacy of certain individuals, names and identifying details have been removed in some of the author's stories, at the request of the publisher.

The stories in this book are intended solely to provide encouragement and motivation to the readers. Neither the author nor the publisher is advocating that any reader follow the medical practices of the people in the stories, nor is any type of medical or professional advice being rendered herein. Each reader should seek his or her doctor's advice about medications and medical treatments. Neither does the author or publisher advocate the general practice of readers putting themselves at risk and/or in harm's way on purpose while taking the Gospel to the streets. Each reader is solely responsible for his or her own choices, actions and results.

Cover design by Studio Gearbox

18   19   20   21   22   23   24   7   6   5   4   3   2   1

"Very truly I tell you, whoever believes in me will do the works I have been doing, and they will do even greater things than these, because I am going to the Father."

John 14:12

This book is dedicated to those the apostle Paul described as "of whom the world was not worthy" (Hebrews 11:38 KJV). My father, consoling my oldest son the first time he was beaten by fellow students for preaching at high school, told him, "You are now a part of a special fellowship, those 'of whom the world is not worthy.' None on the earth may ever know your name, but all of heaven will cheer who you are in this fellowship."

I have stood on platforms to speak before tens of thousands and have had many shout my name after being recognized in airports as I flew back to my safe, comfy home. I sleep soundly tonight as some in this fellowship who are a part of the underground Church sleep with one eye open. None reading here may ever know these precious saints' names, and many will never know their heroism. But all heaven knows, and for a few of them, I know.

I have spent many nights in Iraq, Afghanistan, Iran, Turkey, Armenia and Sri Lanka (to name a few) ministering to people in the shadows or behind objects to conceal us as we passionately shared the love of Jesus with those who had never heard—all the while watching over our shoulders for the secret police or radical terrorist factions to come after us. Members of the persecuted Church bravely took me into their homes, and some were later tortured, robbed or forced to move away because they were found out as believers and advancers of the Kingdom of God. I have wept with them over the loss of fellow laborers who went home too early. On some occasions I have been attacked with them and lost blood myself. And I'll do it again and again and again.

I wish I could name you all here, but that would put you at too great of a risk. But you know who you are, our Father knows you, and I stand with heaven and applaud you. You are heaven's champions. This book is dedicated to you, those "of whom the world is not worthy."

CONTENTS

Contents

FOREWORD

The world all around you is waiting to be transformed. As a matter of fact, it is actually groaning and longing for it (see Romans 8:22). As you grow in your connection to God, you begin to see the wide gap between what He intended this world to be like and how it has veered away from that. Your life then becomes a vehicle to stand in this gap through faith, and your relationship with God incubates the transformation process. As you live a biblical lifestyle of letting the world encounter His love, you will do things that just are not humanly possible or normal—all for the sake of bringing Jesus the full reward He paid for on the cross.

Jesus commissioned His disciples with power and authority and released them to prophesy, heal the sick and cast out demons. They jumped at the chance! They had seen an invasion of His holy love touch the world's brokenness, and when He told them to go and do likewise, their awe of what was possible and their faith to do it set the world on fire.

Then toward the end of His life, Jesus promised His disciples that they would do even greater things than they had seen Him do. His message in John 14:12 was that they had so much more to look forward to and access. Such a great hope—a hope we share, since we now need to access the much more He also has in store for us. *Do Greater Things* will help us in the process.

Robby Dawkins is an activator and equipper who will take you on a journey in this book. There are many teachings and programs, but few are by fathers who live a lifestyle of doing greater things in their family and ministry the way Robby does. Everything you read here comes from the depth of Robby's own life experience, yet at the same time he is never satisfied just to do greater things himself. His love for you and for Jesus compels him to give you the courage, practical teaching, activation steps and stories that will keep you fueled until your own stories and experiences overtake you.

Robby's passionate description of the process of hearing God, dealing with failure and the enemy, and running after the supernatural and a healing ministry is so necessary to read when you need a prototype to show you the way. His vulnerability in telling his stories and sharing the process of growing and overcoming his weaknesses will keep you reading. This book will nurture you like a parent's encouraging words to "Do the Stuff," as the late, great John Wimber, who inspired so many of us (including Robby), would say.

On top of all of this, *Do Greater Things* acts like a training playbook for operating in the gifts of the Holy Spirit. The stories made me laugh, cry and know there is access to more—and then the biblical teaching took me there. Prepare your heart for action as Robby challenges you to do the greater things!

Shawn Bolz, TV personality and author of *God Secrets*,
Translating God and *Growing Up with God*,
www.bolzministries.com

PART ONE

ACTIVATE

1

An Army Is Rising Up

When the seventy-two disciples returned, they joyfully reported to him, "Lord, even the demons obey us when we use your name!"

"Yes," he told them, "I saw Satan fall from heaven like lightning! Look, I have given you authority over all the power of the enemy, and you can walk among snakes and scorpions and crush them. Nothing will injure you."

Luke 10:17–19 NLT

The messages come from all over the United States and from dozens of countries around the world. Emails, texts and letters from excited men, women and children who can't wait to tell me what God is doing in their lives:

Robby, it's true! I did what you said to do, and it works!

Pastor Dawkins, I prayed for a lady who was totally deaf in her left ear, and now she can hear!

The writers are excited about what God has done, and, in some cases, they are stunned that He would choose to do it through them. Many of them tell me that until they read my first book, *Do What Jesus Did* (Chosen, 2013), they thought that God performed miracles and healings only through the hands of very holy and special people. Certainly, they thought, He wouldn't use ordinary, flawed people like them.

But, you know, that's exactly what He does—take it from one who knows. Jesus meant exactly what He said when He told His followers, "Very truly I tell you, whoever believes in me will do the works I have been doing, and *they will do even greater things than these*, because I am going to the Father" (John 14:12, emphasis added).

It's amazing to me that some people are surprised when God does the things He said He'd do. After all, He's God. If He says something, you can bet your life that it's the truth, and there's nothing anyone can do to change it.

Surprised by His Power

Take another look at the passage of Scripture I used at the beginning of this chapter. Can't you just hear the surprise in the disciples' voices? "Lord, even the demons obey us when we use your name!" Before Jesus sent them out, He told them they would have authority over the powers of darkness, but based on what I read in this passage, I can see that they didn't quite believe it. It's as if they're saying, "What You told us is actually true. It really works!"

Of course it does! If you belong to Jesus, you have the power to

- ▶ *heal* the sick
- ▶ *cast out* demons and bring deliverance to those trapped in spiritual darkness

▸ *prophesy* in His name
▸ *call out* creative miracles
▸ *receive* supernatural words of wisdom and knowledge
▸ and even *raise the dead*

Have you heard that inspiring song "Break Every Chain"?[1] My friends at Jesus Culture recorded it. The lyrics talk about the power we have in the name of Jesus and how God is raising up an army that will break every chain. He is on the move all over the world. I know because I've ministered in fifty countries and I've seen it with my own eyes—again and again and again.

If you are in a relationship with Christ, you are in His army. If your heart is stirred to put Jesus on display (as my friend and fellow minister Brian Blount says), then you can be sure that He will put you on display. You can do great things for the sake of His Kingdom if you believe and are willing to step out and take the *risk* (which is another way I often spell faith).

My intent in writing this book is to show you how to activate your faith so you can do even greater things than Jesus and His disciples did—things that will change your community and our world.

A few weeks ago in Scotland, I had the privilege of visiting the gravesite of the great missionary Smith Wigglesworth. Wigglesworth, who preached the Gospel to millions of people throughout the world, was known for the miracles that accompanied his preaching. He healed thousands of sick men, women and children, cast out demons that had held people in bondage for decades, and is said to have raised more than a dozen people from the dead.

As I thought about the life of this great man, I began to consider some of the other great people God has used to change our world. People like John Wimber, Kathryn Kuhlman and

17

Lonnie Frisbee. These are just some of those God has used to show us how to live beyond our expectations and move further and deeper into the realm of His Kingdom. These are the giants whose shoulders we stand on as God uses us to do even greater things for His glory.

The deaths of people like Smith Wigglesworth and Lonnie Frisbee did not bring an end to a great movement of God in these latter days. Their ministries, as great as they were, were only the beginning of a great move of the Holy Spirit that continues today through people like you and me.

I remember how amazed I was when I finished reading Smith Wigglesworth's biography a few years ago. I felt so inadequate in comparison to this great evangelist, and I confessed to God, *I am no Smith Wigglesworth.*

In response, I heard His reassuring voice: *I don't need another Smith Wigglesworth. I need Robby Dawkins now.*

Whoever you may be. Wherever you live. Whatever you may see as your own flaws. God doesn't need another John Wimber or another Kathryn Kuhlman. He needs you!

Who Is Robby Dawkins?

Before we get started on our journey, let me tell you just a little bit about who I am. First of all, I'm a regular person who faces the same daily struggles every human being faces. I have bills to pay and errands to run, children to take care of, and a lawn to mow. I don't go around walking on water, nor do I have a glowing halo floating over my head. The only difference between you and me may be that I am called as a minister and an evangelist. You may or may not share my calling. Whether or not you do, I know that you and I are both called to tell people about the life-changing, transforming love of Jesus. Jesus expects us to heal the sick, cast out demons and even raise the dead in His name!

I'm really an ordinary guy. Yet I have been living a life of miracles from the day I was born. Actually, from before I was born. If you have read either of my previous books, *Do What Jesus Did* or *Identity Thief* (Chosen, 2015), you know that Satan appeared to my mother when she was pregnant with me and told her that he was going to kill me. I won't go further into the details of that story here because, as I said, it has been told before. My point is that I have been aware of God's supernatural, miracle-working power since the early days of my life, so I suppose it's only natural that I would wind up in the Vineyard, a movement that its founder, John Wimber, always said would be totally committed to operating in signs and wonders.

Prior to founding the Vineyard, John and his wife, Carol, attended a church that taught the age of miracles was past. Their church believed that God supernaturally healed the sick and raised the dead through prayer and the laying on of hands way back in the first century, but not anymore. Carol (now a dear friend of ours) told us that one day their toddler son, Sean, encountered a swarm of bees that stung him dozens of times. Ugly red welts covered his body. Fearing for their son's life, the Wimbers placed their hands on him and prayed for his healing. To their amazement, the red splotches on his skin disappeared immediately. They were deeply grateful, and also amazed, that God had answered their prayers.[2]

This was the first of many experiences that convinced the Wimbers that miracles and healings are still available to those who believe. I believe something happened inside John and Carol Wimber on the day their son was attacked by that swarm of bees. Their faith was activated in a new way, and God's power was released to heal their boy. As Christ-following believers, John and Carol had always had the right to call on God and receive healing and miracles from His hand—but they didn't know it. Until that day, they had never cried out for a miracle because they didn't believe miracles were possible. When they spoke in faith, they received.

The same thing can and will happen for you. When you begin to have faith in the power of God, take Him at His Word, understand His love for you and activate it, then you, too, will see His power released in healings, financial blessings and miracles of all kinds.

In *Do What Jesus Did*, I wrote, "This book is not meant to reproduce the Robby Dawkins way of doing things,"[3] which is true of all three of my books. Yet as I witnessed many denominations and movements (even the one I'm in) begin to shift away from the very practices of power that launched them, I felt the need to write a book to declare that God is still on the move and that we can do what Jesus did. My aim with that book was to ignite vision and to encourage and empower people to step out into the things they were created for—"to pitch you the ball and watch each and every one of you knock it out of the park,"[4] as I put it.

When I wrote *Identity Thief*, I built upon that by talking about how the enemy sneaks in and deceives us into thinking we aren't qualified enough, good enough or capable enough for God to use. Satan uses our sins and shortcomings, tempting us with them to keep us out of the batter's box, where the Lord is setting us up to walk in our true identity. That identity in Him is a life filled with love for others as we operate in signs and wonders, reinstating us back into that place of restored relationship with the Father.

My purpose now, in writing *Do Greater Things*, is to build on what I taught in those two books and to further equip you for service in God's Kingdom by helping you move from the batter's box to the pitcher's mound. This means not only stepping out yourself, but also giving away what God has shown you, so that you will see not only your community, but the entire world transformed and engaging in doing what Jesus did. Making that shift activates you as part of the "Spirit Tribe" I will talk more about.

I truly believe this is all part of the *greater things* God is inviting us to in John 14:12. I want to show you how Jesus' power and authority are given to us in practical ways, so that even unbelievers can experience this in action and see how God is inviting them into a relationship with Him. And as you and I demonstrate to others what Jesus is inviting them to in that relationship, it reveals to us that we have more weapons in our arsenal than we realize.

Are you ready to activate the power and presence of Jesus within you, moving wherever He is moving, working with whomever He is working with, doing whatever He is doing? Are you ready to do greater things? Turn the page and let the adventure continue.

YOUR ACTIVATION GUIDE

- ▶ What is the primary benefit you hope to gain from reading this book?
- ▶ What other benefits are you looking for?
- ▶ What does it mean to you to activate your faith?
- ▶ Do you believe and understand that you are one of those who Jesus said would "do greater things"?
- ▶ What can you do to increase your understanding of your worth to God?

2

Greater Things across the World

And the disciples went everywhere and preached, and the Lord worked through them, confirming what they said by many miraculous signs.

Mark 16:20 NLT

Can you imagine a training session in Jesus' healing power taking place inside a mosque in a devoutly Muslim region of Africa, while the imam looks on, smiling and nodding approvingly?

It is hard to imagine, especially in these days of ISIS, terrorists and the open hatred from radical Islamists. But I am writing these words two days after returning home from Sierra Leone, in western Africa, while the miracles I saw there are still fresh in my mind.

Not only did the local mosque leader approve of our worship service, but when other villagers came to pray that afternoon, he turned them away, telling them that he didn't want to interrupt what we were doing because it was so important!

This is yet one more example of the *greater things* Jesus is doing through His followers today.

Sierra Leone is one of Africa's poorest and most dangerous countries. In recent years, the country has been devastated by the deadly Ebola virus, which killed thousands of people and closed off entire communities to the outside world. Another reason why Sierra Leone is dangerous is that the nation is still rebuilding after a long and especially brutal civil war. Rebel soldiers tortured and killed thousands of innocent villagers, and millions more were forced to flee their homes. Hands, arms, legs, noses and ears were chopped off as a warning to others not to support government troops. Today, the country is ostensibly at peace. But you don't want to be out after dark in many of the country's rural areas. And although this predominantly Muslim country is noted for its "religious tolerance," that tolerance fades the farther you get from the big cities, out into the remote areas. As a matter of fact, we had been told to be on our guard, because someone had put poison in the food of some Christian missionaries who had passed through the area a few months earlier. By God's grace, no one died. But they had suffered for several days, and it wasn't an experience we wanted to repeat. So much for tolerance.

I was in Sierra Leone with a small group that included a wonderful woman named Glorious Salamutu Bah, who is a leader with the Vineyard churches in Sierra Leone. My host was my good friend Boris Eichenberger, who brought along several people from a Vineyard church in Switzerland. Glorious herself was beaten and had unspeakable things done to her by rebel soldiers on at least three occasions. She found healing and the ability to forgive by the grace of Jesus, and now she does everything she can to spread His love throughout her native land. She lives out God's style of revenge. Her leadership was unwavering, and every man who knew her respected her, except the husband who had abandoned her and their children. Our group was going out with Glorious to dozens of little rural villages to preach and demonstrate the Gospel and to plant churches where none existed.

A Laugh before the Storm

On the day of the miracle at the mosque, our little group had gone farther than any other day. We drove out into the backcountry as far as we could, much of that time on "roads" that most Americans wouldn't dare tackle, even with four-wheel drive. We traveled over rutted trails strewn with rocks and through sandy stretches that seemed ready to swallow us. I was bouncing up and down so hard and so often that I feared my head was going to crash through the roof of our car, and I'm pretty sure I came close on more than one occasion.

When we reached the place where even our driver didn't think we could go on, I was delighted to get out of the vehicle—even though it meant a long stretch of walking in the heat. My impression is that it's always hot in Sierra Leone. I remember thinking, *When we get to the village, I'm going to find a tree's shade to sit under for a few minutes.* But even in the shade, I figured it was well over 100 degrees.

Our walk to the village was not without incident.

At one point, as we came out into a clearing, we encountered three young women with wet hair, apparently on their way back home after bathing in a local river. One of them, around 25 and very attractive, came over to me, grabbed my arm, pulled it up against her and said, "I like you. I want to marry you."

"Oh, you flatter me greatly, but I can't marry you," I said, trying to extricate my arm. "I'm a very happily married man."

"But you are allowed to have three wives," she said. "I want you to marry me." She tightened her grip on my arm.

I looked around for help, but Boris and the other members of our group were standing there with amused looks on their faces. They were absolutely no help at all.

I turned back to the girl and said, "I can't marry you because I'm old enough to be your father."

"That's even better," she smiled.

"No . . . really, I can't marry you. I have six children and . . ."

"You're breaking my heart," she pleaded, her eyes twinkling mischievously. "Don't say these things. Just tell me you will marry me."

I knew what she was thinking. She saw a white man with some meat on his bones and figured, *He must be a rich guy.* It took some time, but I finally convinced her that I was not in the market for another wife. She looked so sad as my friends and I went on our way, with them all chuckling at my dilemma.

When we finally got to our destination, we found there was no covering where we could set up. In some of the other villages, we had been welcomed into primitive makeshift structures. Some even had benches carved out of logs. Believe me, it was uncomfortable inside those makeshift buildings when they were jammed full of people sitting or standing shoulder-to-shoulder. It truly was like a sauna, but God was always there, opening blind eyes, making tumors disappear, straightening bent legs and backs. Everywhere we went, He showed His abundant love and mercy. How I love the way Jesus generously gives His power.

But, as I said, in this particular village there was no place to meet. There was one decent building in the community, but that was the mosque, which was certainly off-limits to us Christians. As they always do, the African people welcomed us with wide-open arms. Some brought handmade benches or chairs out of their huts for us to use. I was afraid to sit down on any of them. I would never use the word *sturdy* to describe them, and I didn't see one that looked as if it could hold my weight. Our hosts also brought out mangoes for us to eat, showing us their kind hearts and their desire to share what very little they had.

As our group traveled through Sierra Leone, I always looked around for a young girl around the age of eleven or twelve whom I could coach publicly for people who needed healing. If I couldn't find a girl, I would ask a boy of about the same age to come up and help me. I did this because I understand that these Muslim communities operate under an assumption that children are much less important than adults. And because women are regarded as less important than men, girls are at the bottom of the ladder. I wanted to show them that all people are equal in God's eyes, no matter their gender or age. I also felt it was important for them to see that God can and will use anyone who is yielded to Him and willing to be used.

My goal, as always, is to get people to accept Christ as Lord and Savior, and then get them to go out and share Him and His love and power with others in their community.

Jesus Is Welcome in the Mosque

On this day, as on all others, God was with us, and people were amazed to see their neighbors healed through the prayers and the laying on of the hands of a child they all knew as one of their own. Some of the people who were healed that day had been sick and suffering for years, and everyone knew that, too.

While all these wonderful things were going on, I noticed that the imam was watching from a distance. He wasn't smiling, but he didn't look particularly angry either, so it was hard to tell what he was thinking.

As our training went on, I also noticed that the sky was getting darker and darker. Thick black thunderheads were moving in, extremely rare for this time of year. When I felt the first few drops of rain fall on my head, I turned to Glorious and asked, "Is this supposed to be happening?"

"No," she said. "This isn't the rainy season. It almost never rains this time of year."

Despite what she said, the raindrops were getting bigger and closer together as a light sprinkle turned into a steady rain. Soon the steady rain had become a downpour, accompanied by thunder and lightning, and most of the people seemed terrified by the storm. It was only when I thought about it later that I realized why. They were used to weeks without rain, but they were also familiar with torrential rains that washed away just about everything in their village, including their thatched huts. People were looking around, frantic for shelter, but there was no shelter.

Then an idea came to me. How about the mosque? The mosque had a good roof. It had concrete walls. It was the only solidly built building in town.

I found Boris and asked him, "Do you think the imam would let us continue our service in the mosque?"

He smiled at me. "I like the way you think. It couldn't hurt to ask."

But one of the other guys with us said, "Do you have a death wish?"

My friend Boris is handsome, gracious and naturally friendly. He approached the imam and asked, in as nice a way as possible, if our idea was possible. I figured if anyone could convince the imam to let us into the mosque, Boris could.

But he couldn't. He came back shaking his head. "Sorry. He says no way."

There didn't seem to be anything to do but wait out the storm. After a few more minutes of rain, wind and thunder, I decided to try the imam again. We explained that we had come to bring healing in the name of Isa (Jesus), and we reminded him that Isa is referred to in the Qur'an as an honored prophet. We may or may not have suggested to the imam that this would make people want to visit his site more often if he let us in. But I won't say for sure.

The imam agreed. He was not opposed to us talking about Jesus in the mosque. He had refused to allow us inside because the women in our group did not have their heads covered, in accordance with Muslim law. If they covered their heads, they would be allowed inside, although even then, they would have to remain in the back, since women are not allowed into the front area of the building.

We quickly began looking for items the women could use as head coverings. Some ran home for bits of cloth, and others merely pulled off the cloth they had wrapped their breasts with and tied it around their heads like turbans. This meant they were bare-breasted, but that was not a problem, this being rural Africa. The head covering was the most important thing.

Once the issue had been resolved in this way, the imam ushered us into the mosque, where we continued to teach about Jesus. We were administering healing in His name and showing others how to pray for their neighbors and even those in nearby villages. All this time, the imam sat there, smiling and nodding his head in approval.

Several times as the service continued, I expressed thanks to the Father for this amazing miracle of favor. Even if no one had been healed that day, I would have been blown away by the fact that we were standing in a Muslim mosque, worshiping Jesus and preaching salvation through His name. And people *were* being healed. From blindness, deafness, cancer, and diseases and injuries of all types. It was a wonderful day.

Until everything was suddenly interrupted by the loud banging of sticks against the windows. Then suddenly, angry-looking men were peering in at several windows. Some of them were holding big, thick sticks that looked like clubs to me. Others were carrying machetes.

Before we could react, the door burst open and several of the men came inside. I looked over at Boris and saw that he was quietly praying in tongues. Several other people in the room were doing the same thing. So was I!

One of the men stepped forward and shouted, "We've come for prayer, and you are in our building. Why are these women at the front? You shouldn't be here. You need to leave now!"

Everyone fell quiet. The men looked really angry, and I was flashing back to a time many years ago when I was thrown into a prison cell in Russia. As I was being held, I could hear the guard beating the guy in the next cell. By God's hand I was miraculously released. In the mosque, however, I began to wonder, *Will this turn violent?* The last time I had been in Africa, the authorities in Zimbabwe had sent warnings to us that if we persisted in healing the sick publicly and didn't leave town immediately, we would be arrested, beaten and deported. I have been in many such difficult situations, yet I rarely pray for my own safety. I see my well-being as God's responsibility. My responsibility is expanding His Kingdom.

As these thoughts raced through my mind, all of a sudden the imam stood up and held out his hand to stop the men who had ordered us to leave. "No!" he said. "This is good. People are being healed here. They are hearing things they need to hear. We can pray later. You must not interrupt."

The men looked at each other, and I still didn't know what they were going to do. They didn't look happy. But the imam's word was law. They weren't about to oppose him, so they quietly walked away, heading back to their work in the fields.

The imam smiled warmly and said, "Please, continue."

Apparently, some of the men who left even spread the word that the imam approved of what we were doing, because we suddenly had an influx of people who had come to listen and ask for prayer.

At the end of the day, I had an opportunity to speak directly to the imam about the salvation that Christ offers. I asked him if he would like to surrender himself to Jesus, and he said that while he was not ready to do that, we had given him much to think about. He knew that Jesus had shown Himself through the miracles that had been performed in His name.

We finally left that little village as the sun was dipping toward the horizon in the west, grateful for the mercy and grace we had seen God pour out. We had seen Him confirm the Gospel with many signs and wonders that day, and we knew the little portion of Africa we were in would never be the same.

Living in an Age of Miracles

I was visiting with people after preaching in one large American city when a woman came up to me, thrust out her arm and said, "Do you recognize this?"

I wasn't sure what she was talking about. She wasn't wearing a unique bracelet or sporting a tattoo, nor was there anything unusual about her arm.

"Well, you look kind of familiar to me," I said. "But if you're talking about your arm, then, no, I don't recognize it."

"That's probably because when you saw it yesterday, it looked like this." She showed me a photograph on her phone. Apparently, it was a picture of the same arm—but it certainly didn't look the same. It was covered with ugly-looking tumors that made it seem twisted and deformed.

"God told me that when you prayed for me, the tumors would go away. And that's exactly what happened—overnight."

"Praise God!" I said. "I knew your face looked familiar!"

"I was scheduled for surgery to remove this hand and my wrist," she said, holding up her hand. "But after you prayed for me, I didn't need surgery anymore."

As I wrote earlier, God is on the move all over the world. He is pouring out His grace and mercy and setting the captives free from sin, sickness and death.

In a city in India, I prayed for a few Muslim men in a café just a block from the local mosque. (My friends from the area told me not to go there because it was too dangerous, but that made the temptation too strong for me.) Two men were instantly healed. One had severe pain in his chest, and the other had a nasty burn on his leg where the skin had peeled off, but it grew back as we prayed.

Both men had fled in terror afterward, screaming out, "Run, he's a magic man!" I was reminded of how people in Jesus' day accused Him of casting out devils by the power of Beelzebub, prince of devils. Jesus replied, "If a house is divided against itself, that house cannot stand. And if Satan opposes himself and is divided, he cannot stand; his end has come" (Mark 3:25–26).

The two young men who had received healing from God's hand had not heard these words of Jesus. When they tried to sneak back into the café to get the backpacks they had abandoned, I explained to them—and they embraced—that I wasn't doing anything by Satan's power. After all, healing and help for them had come through my hands, but Satan's every act and intention is evil.

After ten or fifteen minutes of sharing, the men asked me to tell them more about "Isa," as Jesus is referred to in the Qur'an. They listened intently and joyfully as I told them about His love for them, and how He had given His life so they might be forgiven of their sins and live with Him forever in heaven.

In another American city, a woman approached me and said she had recently discovered a large lump on the side of her neck. Actually, I knew about it before she told me, because it was about the size of a golf ball and easy to see. It bothered her constantly because it affected her ability to swallow, and she knew that other people were looking at it, even though they tried not to. She had already been to the doctor, who had told her that there was a strong possibility of cancer and had scheduled a biopsy for the following week.

As I touched the mass and commanded it to shrink, I could feel it disappearing under my fingers. I then asked her to check it, and she said it was only about half the size it had been just a few minutes before. I prayed again and felt the lump disappear.

After she checked it, she covered her face with her hands and began to cry. "It's completely gone," she sobbed.

There was nothing left to do but cancel that biopsy. I encouraged her to go back and consult her doctor so he could see the testimony and verify what had happened. Thank You, Jesus!

An Endless Flow

I've already noted that Jesus said His followers would do greater works than He did. He also said, "And I will do whatever you ask in my name, so that the Father may be glorified in the Son. You may ask me for anything in my name, and I will do it" (John 14:13–14). I want to show you how you can activate your faith to open up a never-ending flow of God's power into your life. You can start doing the things that God wants you to do—the same things Jesus did when He was here on earth in the flesh. You can see the sick healed, relationships restored, salvation break in, demons cast out and God's Kingdom expanded.

Anyone who reads the New Testament with an open mind can see clearly that this is the way it was in the early days of the Church. An outpouring of signs and wonders announced the birth of the Church on the Day of Pentecost:

> Suddenly a sound like the blowing of a violent wind came from heaven and filled the whole house where they were sitting. They saw what seemed to be tongues of fire that separated and came to rest on each of them. All of them were filled with the Holy Spirit and began to speak in other tongues as the Spirit enabled them.
>
> Now there were staying in Jerusalem God-fearing Jews from every nation under heaven. When they heard this sound, a crowd came together in bewilderment, because each one heard their own language being spoken.
>
> Acts 2:2–6

Does it make sense to you to believe that it is God's will that the Church He brought into the world through such an amazing display of His power should become little more than a Sunday morning hangout? A place where people catch up on social media through shorter and shorter sermons, long coffee breaks and slick, prerecorded video announcements?

I'm really not trying to be mean; it's just that Jesus said His Church would be advancing in power and storming the gates of hell (see Matthew 16:18). How can we do that if we have no power? He also told us that we are to be the salt of the world, but then He added that if the salt has lost its saltiness, it's useless, and fit only to be cast out and trampled upon (see Matthew 5:13–14). Far too many churches have lost their saltiness. I am convinced that God expects His people to walk in the power of Pentecost.

In the first chapter, I talked about the healing of Sean Wimber after he was stung by a swarm of bees. Sadly, not everyone was as excited about the boy's healing as his parents were. Eventually, because they faced opposition when they talked about their son's healing, they left their church and started a group that evolved into the Vineyard movement. One of the hallmarks of the Vineyard is a belief that when the Gospel is preached, God confirms through signs and wonders the truth of what is being taught. John Wimber wrote,

> Christian signs and wonders are beyond rationality, but they serve a rational purpose: to authenticate the gospel. The gospel is opposed to the pluralistic lie that says all religious experience is equally valid. Signs and wonders validate Christ's sacrifice on the cross and His lordship over every area of our lives.[1]

I believe, as John Wimber did, that, "Signs & wonders are a manifestation of God's love for us. The Resurrection was the greatest sign & wonder of them all and without it our existence would be in vain."[2]

When Peter preached the first public sermon on the Day of Pentecost, he declared, "People of Israel, listen! God publicly endorsed Jesus the Nazarene by doing powerful miracles, wonders, and signs through him, as you well know" (Acts 2:22 NLT).

Acts 14:3 (NLT) says: "But the apostles stayed there [Iconium] a long time, preaching boldly about the grace of the Lord. And the Lord proved their message was true by giving them power to do miraculous signs and wonders."

The second chapter of Hebrews also touches on this:

> How shall we escape if we ignore so great a salvation? This salvation, which was first announced by the Lord, was confirmed to us by those who heard him. God also testified to it by signs, wonders and various miracles, and by gifts of the Holy Spirit distributed according to his will.
>
> Verses 3–4

If We Don't Ask, We Won't Receive

Although some people teach that the age of miracles has ended, I see nothing in the Bible that leads me to believe this is true. In fact, I know from personal experience that it isn't true. God confirmed His Word in the first century by healing the sick, raising the dead, and through the activation of supernatural gifts like prophecy, and words of wisdom and knowledge. God confirms His Word in the 21st century by healing the sick, raising the dead . . . and otherwise doing the very same things that were wrought by the hands of Peter, John, Paul and the other great heroes of the first-century Church.

Why don't we see more miracles in the world today? Because we don't *activate* (act on) the authority Christ gave us . . . and because we don't activate, we don't get miracles and healings. Besides, many leaders of the Church go around telling people that the age of miracles is past. That's why I often say that the Church is the biggest perpetuator of unbelief in the world today. Messages of self-preservation have dominated the Church—sermons on self-improvement and betterment, versus laying down our lives for the Gospel—and that has killed faith. It shouldn't be that way!

As the book of James says, "You do not have because you do not ask God" (James 4:2).

I believe in a God who causes lame people to jump out of wheelchairs and run laps around the sanctuary, a God who instantly opens deaf ears and fills them with sound, a God who instantaneously restores sight to blind eyes. I believe in a God who gives supernatural visions, who imparts knowledge and wisdom through supernatural means, and who raises the dead with a word from His lips. Have we forgotten that we serve a God who parted the Red Sea just in the nick of time to save the Israelites from Pharaoh's soldiers, who shut the mouths of the lions when Daniel was thrown into their den, and who made the flames ineffective when Meshach, Shadrach and Abednego were tossed into the fiery furnace? He caused the sun to stand still in the sky, toppled the walls of Jericho, and enabled a young shepherd boy named David to defeat the mighty giant Goliath in battle. The same God who did all these things—the same God who raised His Son, Jesus Christ, from the dead—is still on the throne today and still performing miracles.

One of the reasons I believe in miracles is because God's Word tells me plainly that they exist. Another reason is because I've seen them happen regularly. I've seen blind eyes open, bent and crippled legs straighten and heal, and hardened gang members and drug dealers weep like babies as they accept Jesus Christ as Lord and Savior. A third reason I believe in miracles is because I get letters like these constantly:

After a meeting at Vineyard Aylesbury, you prayed for healing for my fibromyalgia and constant pain. I felt a flood of warmth all over my body. I went home and put all my medications in the trash bin and declared myself healed in Jesus' name. There were morphine patches, naproxen, amitriptyline, codeine and tramadol. Stopping any of these medications can cause withdrawal, but I had none, and I have not had any pain since then. Praise God!

—Nicola Whittaker

I sprained my right ankle and was instructed to stay off it for two weeks and follow up with my GP in a week. After watching you pray for another girl and seeing her getting healed, I cried to God and asked Him to help me out. He gave me an incredible gift of healing.

—Sally Robinson

Wes's Story

Years ago, when I was starting out in ministry and serving as a youth pastor, a young man with a rather unsavory reputation started coming to our youth group. Wes kind of hung around the edges of the group, occasionally tossing off a wisecrack that resulted in nervous laughter. I tried to talk to him a few times, but he was pretty closed off. I never got the feeling that he was looking down on me because I was "religious," but rather that he was thinking, *You don't know who I am, and when you find out, you won't want to have anything to do with me . . . so don't try to get close to me now.*

Wes was dating one of the girls in our youth group who had grown up in church but was attracted to the "bad boys." He was one of those guys who never let you see who he really was. He hid his true feelings behind a wisecrack or a goofy grin. But the fact that he rarely missed a meeting made me think that he wasn't showing up week after week just because he was looking for customers for his drug dealing. Even though he wouldn't admit it, I believed the message of salvation through faith in Christ that he was hearing again and again must have been taking root in his heart.

Without saying so directly, I tried to let Wes know that I wouldn't kick him out. I wouldn't do that because I knew how much Jesus loved him, just as He loved everyone else in the group. I also sensed that Jesus had an important job for Wes to do. This was true even though I heard from more than one source that he was a drug dealer. Some said he was only coming to youth group because he saw it as a wide-open market for dealing, with no competition. Another reason he came to our group was the hot Christian girlfriend.

At the same time, a young man named Dean, who might have been described as Wes's complete opposite, was also attending the youth group. Wes sat in the back, but Dean was always on the front row. Wes wore T-shirts and jeans hanging below his buttocks, but Dean always showed up in a suit to the youth group—which, frankly, struck me as just a little bit strange since none of the other kids dressed up. Wes knew very little about the Bible, but Dean could give you chapter and verse for just about any topic. I couldn't imagine Wes praying either privately or in public, but Dean seemed to know all the right words and had a knack for using them.

To sum it all up, Wes was kind of a loser who seemed to be headed nowhere—except possibly to jail, whereas Dean was a fine young Christian man with an unlimited future. That's why I was more than a bit shocked when I felt God telling me, *When the time comes for you to leave this church, you'll be handing over your ministry to Wes.*

The thought made me cringe. I was working so hard to teach these kids about living for Jesus. Did He really want me to turn the whole thing over to a petty criminal who would have liked to get them all hooked on drugs? Clearly, God had a lot of work to do before Wes was fit for any sort of position in His Church. Choosing Wes to serve as youth pastor seemed very much like hiring the fox to guard the chickens. But then I thought about how God sees things differently than we do. Plus, if He said it, I could count on it.

Our pastor, who was also my boss, called me into his office one day and told me, "I want you to pour as much time and energy into Dean as you possibly can. God is really going to use that boy someday. In fact, I believe he's going to be the next youth pastor of this church."

That may sound like a put-down, being told by the pastor that he had his eye on a replacement for me, but it wasn't. I was young, just starting out in ministry, and the pastor believed that God was preparing me to be a senior pastor one day. I sat for a moment, trying to think about how I could respond to what he had said without coming across like a troublemaker.

Before I spoke, he said, "You don't seem so enthusiastic."

"Well, Dean seems like a great kid," I began.

"But . . ."

"It's just that I feel God is telling me that Wes will be the next youth pastor."

"Wes!" he shouted in surprise. "That guy's a drug dealer!"

I nodded, "I know."

"He's definitely not going to be the next youth pastor. In fact, I don't even want him in the youth group! I want you to do what you can to get rid of him."

I started to say that Wes needed Jesus, just like all the other kids in the group, but this didn't seem like the time to argue.

"He's a bad influence," the pastor said. "Having him in the group makes it seem as though we're not serious about our commitment to Jesus."

I didn't protest, because I knew that Wes had a bad reputation. But I also knew that Jesus was accused of hanging out with drunkards, prostitutes, tax collectors and other sinners of various kinds, and He responded by saying, "I have not come to call the righteous, but sinners to repentance" (Luke 5:32). Besides, wouldn't the church's reputation get a big boost if people saw Wes turn his life around and start living for God?

When the pastor saw that I honestly believed God had something special in mind for Wes, he still protested, saying I was making a big mistake and wasting my time. He was sure that I somehow must have misunderstood what God had said to me. Only I knew I hadn't.

For the next six months or so, much to our senior pastor's consternation, Wes continued to attend the youth group. His girlfriend was always there, and so was he.

That's when we began planning to host a big event with several other churches from the area. We were going to have a kicking Christian band, a hip-hop dance group from one of the local churches, and a testimony from a well-known

Georgia Tech football player. We expected to fill the place with as many as four hundred teenagers.

As the next youth group meeting was winding up, I approached Wes and asked, "Can I talk to you for a minute?"

He shrugged. "Sure. What about?"

We moved toward a corner where we could talk privately.

"You've heard about this big event we're having?"

"Of course."

"Well, I want you to handle the offering."

A look of horror spread across his face. "Handle the offering? What does that mean? You want me to take money from people?"

"You'll just have to get up in front of the group, say a prayer asking God to bless the offering—"

"I don't think I've ever said a prayer," he interrupted. "About anything. . . ."

"And maybe you can read a Scripture."

"A Scripture?"

"Something about the importance of giving?"

"But I don't know anything about the Bible."

Wes stared at me as if I'd lost my mind. Then his eyes began to sparkle and his mouth curved into a grin. He loved a challenge, and he also loved being the center of attention.

"How many people did you say are going to be here for this thing?"

"Three hundred and fifty. Maybe four hundred."

"All right," he said, "I'll do it!"

"I'm counting on you."

He put his hand on my shoulder. "I won't let you down, dude."

I half expected that he wouldn't even show up for the event, but he did, and he assured me that he was ready to go, even though he seemed a little nervous about it, which surprised me. When the time came, he walked up to the stage in front of the room and stood there with the offering plate in his hands. A smirk played across his lips, as if to say, "Hey everybody, look at me. I bet you never thought I'd be doing something like this, huh?" But through his false bravado, I could see that his hands were trembling. And man, did he have a tight grip on that offering plate! He was playing the same old role of being cocky, but I felt certain that something quite different was going on inside him.

He said, "I'm supposed to read a Bible verse, but I don't really know one, so I'm just going to pray."

He bowed his head and launched into one of the least confident prayers I've ever heard. I can't recall everything he said, but I remember that it started, "God, we know You're there somewhere." When he had finished, he said, "Okay, everybody. You know what this is all about. We're going to pass this plate around, and I want you to put some money in it. And don't be stingy . . . because . . . the church needs the money."

As the offering started to make its way around the room, I noticed that Wes's face wore an expression I had never seen before. The arrogant smirk had given way to an almost tender smile. He looked thoughtful, sober, inspired. I almost thought he was going to cry.

He came down off the stage and sat next to me.

"What did you do to me?" he asked.

"What do you mean?"

"Something happened to me when I was up there." He jerked his head in the direction of the stage. "I want to know what it was."

"Well, Wes," I smiled, "I just gave you a vision of your future."

He shook his head. "I don't get it."

"God has plans for you," I told him. "You're going to preach the Gospel. You're going to lead young people to Jesus. You're going to be the youth pastor of this church."

He looked down at the floor and began to tremble. "I know that's true," he said.

I asked him if he wanted to give his life to Jesus, but he shook his head. "I'm just not ready," he said, and then repeated it in a whisper. *"I'm just not ready."*

A few days later, he came back to the church and sought me out. "I just can't forget what happened to me up there on the stage," he told me. "I've tried to get it out of my mind and heart, but I can't."

"Are you ready to surrender your life to Jesus?" I asked him.

"I am."

There in my office, he bowed his head and I led him in a short prayer of surrender to Christ.

When we finished praying, tears were running down the tough guy's cheeks. And something else had happened. Wes had always had a problem with acne. It was one of the first things I noticed about him when I saw him for the first time. But now, in an instant, his pimples were gone! His face was as smooth as the skin of a newborn baby. God had given a sign to Wes that something real had happened to him, a "wonder" to verify the truth of the Gospel.

It might sound like a cliché, but from that day forward, Wes really was a different person. The smart remarks were replaced by serious, honest comments and questions. He stopped selling drugs. He was still a little rough around the edges, but he was being transformed into the likeness of Christ.

Just as God had told me would happen, when the time came for me to move on from that church, Wes was ready to move into my position of youth pastor. And he did a marvelous job.

What had happened to Wes? The tiny spark of faith that burned inside him had been ignited into a roaring flame. As he stood on that stage with the collection plate in his hand, the Holy Spirit had shown him beyond any doubt that Jesus was real and loved him more than he had ever thought anyone could or would. He also saw his need for God in his life, and I believe he really understood, for the first time ever, who he really was—not a drug dealer! A valued, loved son with incredible leadership abilities, who had not been aware that he was chosen by Christ. Wes is a dear friend to this day.

Activate Your Faith

Such moments of decision come to all of us. We must decide whether or not to accept Jesus as Lord and Savior and receive the Kingdom authority He has given us. Then we must decide to move forward into a Spirit-activated life. After that, we must make decisions every day about whether to do things Jesus' way or our way.

All who have given their lives to Christ have the Holy Spirit within them. On the day you accepted Jesus as your Lord and Savior, you received the Holy Spirit. The flame of the Spirit is burning within you, like the pilot light of your hot water heater. But you have to ask God to fan that little light in you and turn it into a blaze so that it can do what it's supposed to do. Now, understand that I am not comparing God to something as mundane as a water heater. But think about it. That pilot light was designed as the means of providing hot water to your entire house. But if you don't turn it up, you'll never have anything but cold water, and your morning shower will be a most unpleasant experience—especially in the winter.

How do you turn that pilot light into a flame and activate the power of the Holy Spirit within you? You spend time every day thanking God for filling you to overflowing with His Holy Spirit. Then you enthusiastically expect Jesus to shine out of you for His Kingdom and His glory. In Luke 11:11–13, Jesus says,

Which of you fathers, if your son asks for a fish, will give him a snake instead? Or if he asks for an egg, will give him a scorpion? If you then, though you are evil, know how to give good gifts to your children, how much more will your Father in heaven give the Holy Spirit to those who ask him!

Here are three important truths we all need to remember:

- ► If you ask God to forgive your sins, He will.
- ► If you ask Him to fill you with the Holy Spirit, He will.
- ► If you step out for Him to use you, He will.

The Bible says that on the first night Jesus appeared to the apostles after His resurrection, He breathed on them and told them, "Receive the Holy Spirit" (John 20:22). He then said they had received the power to forgive sins on earth. They had to take it by faith that this was true, because there were no visible signs that anything had happened. It was a solemn, thought-provoking night for Christ's followers, and it stayed that way.

Then, just prior to His ascension into heaven, the Lord told the apostles to wait in Jerusalem until the Holy Spirit came upon them.

What? I thought they had already received the Holy Spirit, you might think.

They had! But if that's so, what happened on the Day of Pentecost, when Jerusalem was filled with the sound of a mighty, rushing wind, when tongues of fire burned on the apostles' heads, and when they spoke in supernatural languages? On the first occasion, Jesus' followers received the gift of the indwelling Spirit, a drink of the living water that Jesus gives at the moment we accept Him as Lord and Savior. On the second, they were immersed in the Holy Spirit, who gave them the power to utilize the supernatural gifts He provides.

If you belong to Jesus, if you have accepted Him as the Savior of your soul and the Lord of your life, you have the same power within you that was unleashed on the Day of Pentecost. But it is up to you to activate it. Too many believers are hiding their light under a bushel. Now, more than ever, we must let His love and power shine through us.

Signs and Wonders Made Simple

Let me assure you again that God can and will use you if you activate what He has given you. It doesn't matter who you are, how old you are or whether you are a powerful person in the eyes of the world. Remember, God used a shepherd kid, David, to defeat a powerful giant named Goliath. And Samuel was just a child when God spoke to him in the middle of the night and told him that he was going to bring judgment on the high priest and his family. Mary, who gave birth to our Messiah, was most likely only about fourteen years old when the great event of His birth occurred.

Look at what the Bible says:

> In a large house there are articles not only of gold and silver, but also of wood and clay; some are for special purposes and some for common use. Those who cleanse themselves from the latter will be instruments for special purposes, made holy, useful to the Master and prepared to do any good work.
>
> 2 Timothy 2:20–21

God often chooses the most unimposing among us to serve as vessels of His great power. This is one reason I often call on children and youth whom I can coach when I pray for the sick in public meetings. I rarely pray for anyone publicly in a church or conference anymore. I've become weary of long lines of people who only want me to pray for them after meetings.

I fear they've missed the point that this is not about some special anointing that I have, but rather about the power and authority Christ gives to all believers.

In the Dominican Republic earlier this year, I was doing a School of Power and Love[3] with my dear friends Todd White and Tom Ruotolo. I called a teenage boy to come up on stage to pray for a woman who was suffering because one of her legs was significantly shorter than the other.

There were more than eight hundred people in the auditorium at the time, and the service was being shown on several large screens via a live camera feed. I also asked the cameraman to come over and get as close as he possibly could with a straight-down shot so that the entire audience would get an excellent view of the woman's leg growing out. (By the way, always watch the heels when you're doing this, as that's where you can see legs grow.)

Meantime, I asked the young man if he had ever prayed for somebody and seen the person healed.

"No, never," he replied.

"Well, I'm going to have you pray for this woman."

I first asked the woman to slip her shoes off. (I don't always do this, but because I've seen magicians do fake leg growings by shifting the heel of the shoe out, sometimes I do now.) I then asked him to get down on his knees and hold her legs with the heels touching each other. Then I led him in a repeat-after-me style of prayer for her healing.

Nothing happened.

Then I basically told him to thank the Lord and command the leg to grow in Jesus' name.

Still nothing.

I have to admit, I was feeling a little nervous for the boy, what with that TV camera poised to show a healing miracle and that leg demonstrating all the vitality of a still-life painting.

I then asked the boy to repeat after me as I said, "By the authority of Christ, I bind every attack of the enemy, and I command all resistance to stop now. . . ."

Boom, her leg grew out just like that. The movement was as clear as could be, as the leg moved out and became the same length as the other leg. Her heels were now exactly even! You could hear the excitement in the audience: *"Ooooh, aaaah!"* It was like being at a major-league baseball game where someone makes a great fielding play, or lines a triple into the corner with the bases loaded.

The lady got up and gracefully walked around the stage. She moved as free and easy as could be, wiping away the tears that had come because she was moving without pain in her back and hips for the first time in years.

When I asked her to describe what had happened, she said, "It felt as if someone were pulling my leg, getting it to go into the right position. But it wasn't this young man. He was just lightly holding them—they were resting on his hands. Then I felt a surge of something like electricity passing through my body."

Give as You Have Received

The woman whose leg grew out later told me that she had come to the conference just to listen to the teaching and not to get involved in any other way. But after what had happened to her, she couldn't wait to get out and pray for others. She had received freely. Now she wanted to give freely. When we went out into the streets to pray for people, she was in the forefront of the action. Many were healed and delivered through her prayers, and through the prayers of the young man who had prayed for her leg to grow out.

That night, the pastor of the church that was hosting the conference called the overseer of his denomination and told him, "You have to come here and see this! We're seeing some incredible manifestations of the Holy Spirit."

The overseer came, saw what God was doing, and experienced God's power in a mighty way.

After I spoke that night, inviting the Holy Spirit's presence and power to fall on us, the overseer told me, "It's been many years since I've felt that much power rushing through my body. And I realized it was something the Lord was giving to me so that I could give to others. I had never thought of it that way until I heard you say that we are being filled up to be poured out."

The pastor also came to thank me for showing his congregation how simple it is to do the works of God.

"In our minds, I think we had made it too complicated," he said. "We had come to think that there were only certain people who had the power to heal the sick or cast out demons. But you showed us that we can all do those things."

Yes, we can. And it is simple, if you only believe and *activate*!

The Scripture below applies to you, just as surely as it applied to the Christians at Ephesus nearly two thousand years ago:

I pray that the eyes of your heart may be enlightened in order that you may know the hope to which he has called you, the riches of his glorious inheritance in his holy people, and his incomparably great power for us who believe. That power is the same as the mighty strength he exerted when he raised Christ from the dead and seated him at his right hand in the heavenly realms, far above all rule and authority, power and dominion, and every name that is invoked, not only in the present age but also in the one to come. And God placed all things under his feet and appointed him to be head over everything for the church, which is his body, the fullness of him who fills everything in every way.

Ephesians 1:18–23

YOUR ACTIVATION GUIDE

- ▶ How did you come to faith in Christ? Write about it in an email and send it to yourself so you can always read it. It will help build and activate your faith.

- ▶ Have you ever seen someone supernaturally healed from a devastating illness? If so, tell others about it or meditate on it and remind yourself that God can do the very same thing through you.

- ▶ Why do you think God would choose to use a kid like Wes? What can we all learn from this?

- ▶ What, if anything, holds you back from going out onto the streets and doing what Jesus did?

- ▶ Have you ever spent time with Jesus, just asking Him to hold you? Set aside at least ten minutes every day this week to sit in His presence, basking in His love, mercy and power.

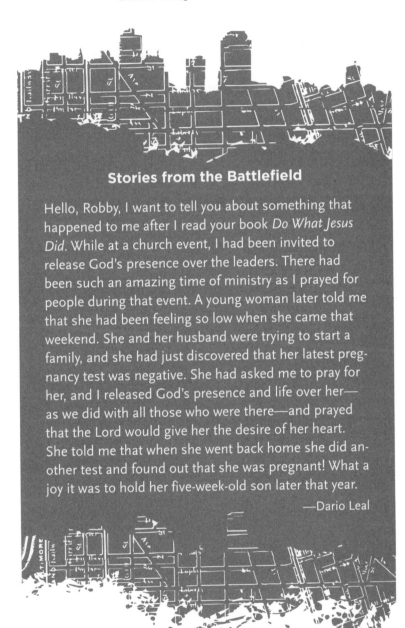

Stories from the Battlefield

Hello, Robby, I want to tell you about something that happened to me after I read your book *Do What Jesus Did*. While at a church event, I had been invited to release God's presence over the leaders. There had been such an amazing time of ministry as I prayed for people during that event. A young woman later told me that she had been feeling so low when she came that weekend. She and her husband were trying to start a family, and she had just discovered that her latest pregnancy test was negative. She had asked me to pray for her, and I released God's presence and life over her— as we did with all those who were there—and prayed that the Lord would give her the desire of her heart. She told me that when she went back home she did another test and found out that she was pregnant! What a joy it was to hold her five-week-old son later that year.

—Dario Leal

PART TWO

SPIRIT TRIBE

3

Heal the Sick
in the Name of Jesus

Heal the sick, raise the dead, cleanse those who have leprosy, drive out demons. Freely you have received, freely give.

Matthew 10:8, emphasis added

named this next part of the book Spirit Tribe because my dear friend Craig Simonian—who has served as a missionary to Tazjikistan for years and is now moving to Armenia—started a group called Spirit Tribe. And together, we are working on developing a School of Supernatural Ministry that will impact Muslim nations with signs and wonders to bring them to Jesus. Spirit Tribe is made up mostly of young people who are willing to band together in tribes to bring the love of Jesus to a particular people group or area. Tribe members must be willing to integrate into their community—even going so far as being willing to lay their lives down for the Gospel—to see peoples or nations transformed by the power of the Holy Spirit.

As Romans 14:7–8 (NLT) says, "For we don't live for ourselves or die for ourselves. If we live, it's to honor the Lord. And if we die, it's to honor the Lord. So whether we live or die, we belong to the Lord." Revelation 12:11 (NLT) says, "And they have defeated him by the blood of the Lamb and by their testimony. And they did not love their lives so much that they were afraid to die."

Let me illustrate. My son Judah, who was then sixteen, and one of his young, homeless friends from church were preaching the Gospel and praying for people in a downtown business district of our city. (Our church was in a poor urban community, so we had many homeless members.) Judah and his friend didn't really realize it, but they had set up shop in front of a large corporate office, which shall remain nameless. As they ministered the love of Jesus, a bit of a crowd began to gather. That's when a woman who had suffered a great deal of back pain because one leg was significantly shorter than the other came for prayer. As Judah and his 25-year-old homeless buddy called out for passersby to stop and watch, they laid hands on her and began to pray. Her short leg grew out in a visible way, the bone popping and cracking as the limb extended.

The woman was filled with joy and wonder as people watched what was going on. When they heard her praising God for the miracle she had received and saw the tears of joy streaming down her face, others began crowding around, asking for prayer.

"I have arthritis. Will you pray for me?"

"I just found out I have cancer."

"I ruptured a disk."

"Of course we'll pray for you," Judah said. "Jesus loves you, and He wants you to be well."

It's not too often you see a spontaneous healing event take place on the downtown streets of an American city. But this was a typical experience for Judah and his friends, who were following the example of the first-century disciples and preaching the Gospel with an expectation that God would confirm His Word through a demonstration of signs and wonders.

But, as in Jesus' day, not everyone approved of what God was doing.

"What do you think you're doing?" a man shouted. "Stop that right now!"

Judah turned and saw that an impeccably dressed older man in a dark suit had come out of the building and was sprinting toward them. His face was almost as red as the necktie he wore, which had flipped over his left shoulder—and he looked angry. A name tag on his left breast pocket identified him as someone important.

"This is private property!" he yelled. "You're not allowed to do this here."

Judah started to explain that they were on a public sidewalk, but the man wouldn't let him talk. "Get out of here now!" he shouted.

The man's eyes looked wild. He was way too angry.

Judah was suddenly aware that he was dealing with more than natural anger. He was convinced that this executive was under demonic influence. He pointed at the man and shouted, "You have a demon inside you! Come out of him in the name of Jesus, you foul demon!"

The man gasped and then tumbled backward to the ground, as if he had been hit by an electric shock. The two young men ran to him, binding the spirit in Jesus' name. The man's chest lunged forward, he coughed a few times, and then he started panting heavily.

He lay there for at least a minute and then got up with a complete change of demeanor and countenance. He apologized to the boys and asked their forgiveness. When they told him he needed to accept Jesus into his life, he readily agreed to pray with them. After that, he woozily made his way back into the building. Then Judah and his friend continued sharing the love of Jesus and praying for people—many of whom were healed. Some commented, "So, that was a demon? Yeah, I could see that."

A couple of weeks later, Judah's homeless friend brought some other people from another church to do ministry in the same downtown business district. As they were praying and asking the Holy Spirit for direction, a well-dressed young lady with tears in her eyes approached them.

"Are you the guys who were down here praying for people a few weeks ago?" she asked.

"That was us," he told her.

"Well, I'm just wondering . . ." She stepped closer. "What did you do to my boss?"

"Excuse me?"

"You did something to my boss. He came out of our building yelling at you, and then it looked as if he fell or something."

They smiled. "He had an encounter with God."

"Well, whatever it was, it changed him," she stated. "He hasn't been the same at all."

"Really?"

"He used to be the meanest man in the world," she said. "As far as he was concerned, I couldn't do anything right. None of us could. He was constantly on our backs about everything."

She shook her head. "But ever since you prayed for him—or whatever you did—he couldn't be sweeter. He's constantly telling me how much he appreciates all the work I do. He compliments me on my work . . . and he never did that before. He really is a changed man. Could you guys give that same thing to me?"

"We sure can," they said, and they prayed with her to receive Christ.

As Alfred Lord Tennyson wrote, "More things are wrought by prayer than this world dreams of."

You Have More Power than You Realize

How do you heal the sick, deliver people from demonic torment and raise the dead?

You pray for them, commanding transformation.

That really is the bottom line. As the story I just told you illustrates, the prayer of authority moves opposition.

If you don't speak to the condition, no healing will take place.

If you do pray with authority, God has already responded to that prayer at the cross and now amazing things will happen. The Bible is clear:

> You who answer prayer, to you all people will come.
>
> Psalm 65:2

> Ask and it will be given to you; seek and you will find; knock and the door will be opened to you. For everyone who asks receives; the one who seeks finds; and to the one who knocks, the door will be opened.
>
> Matthew 7:7–8

> Again, truly I tell you that if two of you on earth agree about anything they ask for, it will be done for them by my Father in heaven.
>
> Matthew 18:19

> If you believe, you will receive whatever you ask for in prayer.
>
> Matthew 21:22

Therefore I tell you, whatever you ask for in prayer, believe that you have received it, and it will be yours.

Mark 11:24

You may ask me for anything in my name, and I will do it.

John 14:14

If you remain in me and my words remain in you, ask whatever you wish, and it will be done for you.

John 15:7

All but one of these Scriptures are Jesus' instructions to the disciples in prayer before He went to the cross. I believe these verses illustrate prayers being in relationship.

Someone says, "But I don't know how to pray."

Well, I have seen some of the least polished and articulate prayers produce amazing results. Prayer is having a conversation with God, not giving an oration. Jesus often went out into the wilderness and spent the entire night praying to God. Don't you wish you could have been there to hear some of those conversations between Father and Son? What emotion and passion and honesty there must have been in those prayers! Jesus was not out there making speeches to His heavenly Father. He was engaged in a conversation that went on for hours. Do you remember what it was like when you first fell in love with your wife or husband? Most of us spent hours talking on the phone every night. We just couldn't get enough of time spent with the person we loved. Sometimes, the conversation would end like this:

"I guess it's time for me to get to bed. But you hang up first."

"No, you hang up first."

"No, you."

And so it would go. Perhaps that sounds a bit silly to you now. Maybe you can't imagine being on the phone for that long. If you've been married a long time, you may not be able to imagine your spouse hanging on to your every word like that. But prayer provides us with the means of having that type of "I can't get enough of you" relationship with God. It seems to me that anyone who loves the Lord will naturally want to spend time with Him in prayer. If prayer is difficult for you, then ask God to help you love Him more.

I love this thought from Joyce Meyer: "Spending time with God is the key to our strength and success in all areas of life. Be sure that you never try to work God into your schedule, but always work your schedule around Him."[1]

If you struggle with prayer, remember that God listens to your heart more than He does the words you use. In fact, the Bible tells us that when we don't know how we should pray, the Holy Spirit intercedes on our behalf:

> We do not know what we ought to pray for, but the Spirit himself intercedes for us through wordless groans. And he who searches our hearts knows the mind of the Spirit, because the Spirit intercedes for God's people in accordance with the will of God.
>
> Romans 8:26–27

Paul, who wrote the above words, also wrote that he had prayed three times for God to remove the "thorn in the flesh" that troubled him constantly and apparently made him feel he was less effective as a leader. But God responded, "My power is made perfect in weakness" (2 Corinthians 12:9). This is supported by the passage from the book of Exodus, where God called Moses to go to Pharaoh and demand that he free the Hebrew slaves. Moses complained that God should get someone else to do it because "I have never been eloquent, neither in the past nor since you have spoken to your servant. I am slow of speech and tongue" (Exodus 4:10).

And how did God respond? "Who gave human beings their mouths? Who makes them deaf or mute? Who gives them sight or makes them blind? Is it not I, the LORD? Now go; I will help you speak and will teach you what to say" (Exodus 4:11–12).

Attracted to God's Power

I admit that some people get very uncomfortable when I talk about signs and wonders. They tell me that people don't like "displays of emotionalism," and that they are frightened and driven away by displays of God's supernatural power. Some have quoted 1 Corinthians 14:40 (KJV) to me, "Let all things be done decently and in order." But "decently and in order" doesn't mean "dull, boring and devoid of the Spirit."

People are not repelled by God's power, but attracted by it.

We just looked at how Jesus prayed for His disciples before He went to the cross and before the Holy Spirit had been poured out at Pentecost. Now look at this passage from James, which illustrates a style quite different that takes place *after* Pentecost. A new authority had been released that Jesus promised would rest on His apostles:

> And the prayer offered in faith will make the sick person well; the Lord will raise them up. If they have sinned, they will be forgiven. . . . The prayer of a righteous person is powerful and effective.
>
> James 5:15–16

The gospels report that multitudes of people constantly followed Jesus, attracted by the words He spoke and the miracles He performed. On the Day of Pentecost, when the Holy Spirit fell on the apostles in Jerusalem, a crowd also came together to see what was happening (see Acts 2:6). The fifth chapter of Acts reports that "crowds gathered also from the towns around

Jerusalem, bringing their sick and those tormented by impure spirits, and all of them were healed" (verse 16). Crowds also gathered when Judah and his friends were praying for people to be healed in that downtown business district.

I'll say it again: A display of God's power brings people together so they can hear God's Word being taught. My dear friend Brian Blount calls this "putting Jesus on display." The Bible says again and again that God gives us His power:

> I will not venture to speak of anything except what Christ has accomplished through me in leading the Gentiles to obey God by what I have said and done—by the power of signs and wonders, through the power of the Spirit of God.
>
> Romans 15:18–19

> For the kingdom of God is not a matter of talk but of power.
>
> 1 Corinthians 4:20

> Finally, be strong in the Lord and in his mighty power.
>
> Ephesians 6:10

> For the Spirit God gave us does not make us timid, but gives us power, love and self-discipline.
>
> 2 Timothy 1:7

Luke 6:19 says that just before Jesus gave His Sermon on the Mount, "the people all tried to touch him, because power was coming from him and healing them all."

The same power is available to us today.

Marilyn's Story

I met Marilyn Anderson and her husband, Ron, at a Power and Love conference in Lexington, Kentucky. I was impressed right away with their faith and love for God. Marilyn's eyes sparkled with the joy of her love for the Lord. I never would have suspected that she was battling stage 4 bone cancer. She had been undergoing powerful chemotherapy at Duke University, and they had driven all the way from North Carolina to attend the conference.

Despite the smile on her face, Marilyn was in severe pain. She told me later that she could barely turn her head from side to side. Before I prayed for her healing, I asked her—as I almost always do—to rate her pain level on a scale of 1 to 10. As I recall, it was an 8.

As soon as I finished praying, she excitedly told me it had fallen all the way to 0.

"Are you sure?" I asked. "Don't be nice to me."

"I'm not!" she laughed. "The pain is gone."

"Move your head and see how it feels."

"It feels fine," she said, bending her neck backward and forward and from side to side.

We praised God together, and then Marilyn and her husband went off to have lunch before the afternoon sessions began.

As they sat together in their booth at the restaurant, rejoicing over what God had just done for Marilyn, Ron told her, "I feel like my bones are singing."

Her mouth fell open in surprise. "It's so amazing that you said that," she told him. "I was just going to say the same thing to you."

Marilyn tells me that when the service started that afternoon, the first song the worship team led said something about our hearts crying out and our bones singing. The Andersons had never heard the song before. But as Marilyn sang those words, she knew beyond any doubt that God had reached down in mercy and cleansed her body of every cancerous cell, as we had prayed earlier.

A Message from the Messiah

Just before King Herod executed him, John the Baptist sent some of his disciples to Jesus to ask Him if He was, indeed, the Messiah: "Are you the one who is to come, or should we expect someone else?" (Matthew 11:3).

Jesus told John's disciples to go back to their teacher and tell him what they had seen: "The blind receive sight, the lame walk, those who have leprosy are cleansed, the deaf hear, the dead are raised, and the good news is proclaimed to the poor" (verse 5).

Jesus clearly presented the healings and miracles He was performing as a sign that the Kingdom of God had come.

Yes, it is also true that Jesus said that a "sinful and adulterous" generation looks for a sign (see Matthew 12:39; 16:4). But these words were directed at those whose motives were impure and who never seemed satisfied. As soon as Jesus performed one miracle, they wanted to see another—and they wanted it to be greater and grander than the previous one. They were looking for a good show and nothing more.

But Jesus also said, "For the works that the Father has given me to finish—the very works that I am doing—testify that the Father has sent me" (John 5:36). And He said, "Do not believe me unless I do the works of my Father. But if I do them, even though you do not believe me, believe the works, that you may know and understand that the Father is in me, and I in the Father" (John 10:37–38).

As I said before, if you belong to Jesus, the power of God is within you. It's the same power that parted the Red Sea so the Israelites could pass through, the same power that gave Elijah a resounding victory over the priests of Baal and the same power that raised Jesus Christ from the dead. God has given us His power, and now He expects us to use it for His glory. How do we do that? By asking Him to fill us to overflowing with His Holy Spirit, and then by stepping out believing it's there.

Here is one of the primary reasons why we don't see more people moving in the power of God: *We are afraid of looking stupid.*

"Robby," someone asks, "what if I pray for someone to be healed and nothing happens?"

Well, first of all, that's God's business. I often say that another way to spell faith is *r-i-s-k*. If you believe in God and trust that He will work through you, He will! Yes, there have been times when I have prayed for people and didn't get the results I wanted. Almost always, it was a temporary setback that came because there was something I was growing in, or because the person I was praying for had something to learn to release. I never know what is going to happen when I pray for someone, but I relax in the knowledge that God is giving His all for all involved. You can know that, too. You don't have to worry about the results. The results are for Him and not us! For me to get upset when we don't experience the desired result would be like saying the glory is for me when something does result. It's not!

Even on those occasions when I've prayed for someone and we haven't seen an immediate response, nobody got mad at me. No one yelled at me or told me I was a failure. Instead, they appreciated the fact that I had cared enough to pray for them. Even if some people tell you they don't want you to pray for them, most people will appreciate the offer.

Many years ago, I was at a church in the mountains of the Dominican Republic when God gave me a word for a young teenage boy. I'll call him Rodrigo.

I asked Rodrigo, "Do you like music?"

He shook his head. "Not really."

"Do you sing or play the guitar?"

Again, his answer was no.

"That's really strange," I said, "because I see that you're going to write songs, play the guitar and be a worship leader for God's glory in front of many people."

The boy just smiled and shook his head at me, as if he couldn't quite believe what he was hearing.

I would have been content to leave it there, but God wasn't finished. "God says you're going to be known throughout the Dominican Republic for your music."

The boy kept staring at me with a blank look on his face, and I could see that he was having trouble making sense of what I had said.

After the service that day, his pastor, who was joining us from another church, gently told me, "I'm afraid you really missed the mark with that prophecy you gave to Rodrigo."

"I just told him what I sensed God showing me," I responded.

"Have you ever heard him sing?" the pastor asked.

"No."

"Take it from me—he can't and he shouldn't."

I wasn't really puzzled by this, because I knew that all things are possible with God. Then, as time went by, I forgot about it.

A couple of years later, Rodrigo's pastor invited me back to the Dominican Republic, but this time to his church. A young man with a beautiful tenor voice was playing the guitar and leading the worship team in some lovely songs I had never heard before.

"What do you think of our worship leader?" the pastor asked me."

"He's very good," I replied.

"Do you recognize him?"

"No. Should I?"

"That's Rodrigo," he said.

"Rodrigo?"

At first, the name didn't ring a bell.

"Yes, Rodrigo. You told him he was going to be a singer."

"Oh, yes! I remember. What happened?"

A grin spread across the pastor's face. "He couldn't sing. And then all of a sudden after your word, he could! Then he learned to play the guitar. And he writes all his own songs, too."

When I talked to Rodrigo later, I learned that other churches in the Dominican Republic were using his songs and he was in the process of recording his first CD. What had seemed like a big mistake on my part was not really a mistake at all. As was the case with Wes, the young man who replaced me as youth pastor, I had heard God correctly.

When my mother was seriously ill with cancer, I heard clearly from the Holy Spirit that the time had come to let her go. He showed me the exact date, even to the minute, when she would die. So, even though I wanted to see her get well, I no longer prayed for physical healing, but rather for strength, peace and relief from suffering, not only for her, but for my father and our family, too. One night before the Lord showed me when my mother would die, she told me that she was ready to go home. It was as if she released herself in the throes of the battle, rather than cancer stealing her life.

Take Prayer Out of the Church

I said earlier that God can't answer our prayers if we never pray. I also believe we are missing the full effectiveness of prayer if we keep it within the Church—in other words, if we only pray for our fellow believers.

Of course, I believe it's good to pray for other Christians. The book of James tells us to "confess your sins to each other and pray for each other so that you may be healed" (James 5:16). But I also believe the true life-changing power of prayer is more clearly demonstrated when we pray for unbelievers. There are two reasons for this: 1) Answered prayer is a confirmation of the truth of the Scriptures and the Lordship of Jesus; 2) Satan has declared war on the Church and is more determined to hang on to any harm he can cause in a believer's life. For this reason, he has dispatched his best "soldiers" to cause as much havoc among God's people as he possibly can. I can't give you a specific chapter and verse for this, but it has been my experience that you have to fight harder to bring healing to those who already belong to Jesus.

As John Wimber used to say, "The meat's in the street." What he meant was that God wants us to take His power to the millions of people who are lost and living in the world. Too many churches are "preaching to the choir," giving all of their ministry to those who are already saved. We look at the Church as if it's a type of ark to shelter saved people from the dangers of the world. Instead, it should be an equipping center that sends us out to change the world for Jesus.

My point is that we are missing out on much of what God wants to do if we keep our prayers confined within the four walls of the church building.

Look for Opportunities

Opportunities to pray for people are all around you. Some of those opportunities may be obvious. Look for opportunities to heal, deliver and prophesy. If you see someone who is limping along, shuffling along because of a bad back, or suffering from obvious physical pain, that person needs prayer.

But just about everyone has needs that we can't see. People may be struggling in their marriage or other relationships, dealing with sickness in their family, struggling to pay their bills, or battling an illness not necessarily visible at a glance, such as cancer or heart disease.

Sometimes, if we keep our ears open, God will reveal to us that a person has a specific need we are supposed to pray for. When He does that, it's because He is in relentless pursuit of that person, and it's important to let the person know. The worst that could happen is that you'll be wrong—or the person may tell you that you're wrong because he or she is embarrassed. But I have found that as I've become more accustomed to hearing God's voice, I've reached the point where I am seldom wrong. If you are fairly new at this process of walking in signs and wonders, and as you begin to step out in faith in this way, you will find that God begins to reveal the deeper needs of the people you meet each day.

My friend Shawn Bolz has an amazing prophetic gift. He gets people's addresses, parts of phone numbers and on and on. But what I love so much about Shawn is his humility and simple understanding that God is revealing stuff about someone because He wants to let that person know how much He loves him or her. Shawn's book *Translating God: Hearing God's Voice for Yourself & the World around You* (ICreate Productions, 2015) is filled with amazing stories of encounters that have taken place on planes and in grocery stores and coffee shops. I love watching Shawn knock it out of the park. But I've also seen him get it wrong. The amazing thing is, even when he misses it, that doesn't lessen his message to people that "Jesus loves you and wants to have a relationship with you." That message is never wrong!

On the other hand, there are times when it seems that God is silent. Then you just have to ask a person if he or she has a special need you can pray for.

Am I saying you should go around asking everyone you meet if you can pray for them? Why not! I have a former PA (personal assistant) who spends a lot of time hanging around handicapped parking places. (And there are hundreds of these in every city throughout North America.) When he sees someone getting out of a car in one of these spaces, he'll go up and politely ask, "Where do you need healing?"

Now, it's true that some of these people hurry past him as if they don't have a thing in the world wrong with them—and they may not. Others say that they don't need or want prayer, and occasionally they are quite rude about it, although not all that often. But he has seen a number of people healed and saved. Surely, it's worth risking a little abuse now and then to see lives won for God's Kingdom. There's never a time when it's not okay to step out in faith and pray.

One time, I was having a meeting with a businessman who was helping me with my finances, and I noticed that he kept favoring his right shoulder. "Something wrong with your shoulder?" I asked him.

"Yeah," he said, "I injured it playing sports in high school, and it has hurt me ever since." He extended his arm and turned it from side to side. "Pretty much all the time."

"Would you allow me to pray for you?"

He scooted back in his chair, obviously taken aback.

"Pray for me? What are you—some kind of faith healer?"

"Well," I smiled, "I have faith. And I know that God can heal. So, yeah, I guess that makes me a faith healer."

He looked around, as if to see if anyone else was watching. "I don't know."

"Jesus will heal you right now, and you'll never deal with that pain again. I guarantee you."

"How do you know that?"

"I just do."

The truth was, I never have guarantees. I was stepping out in faith, cranking up the risk (as I put it). But I chose to believe that Jesus meant it when He said that He would give us whatever we asked for in His name.

"Okay, I guess it couldn't hurt," he said.

I said a short prayer, commanding the pain to leave in the name of Jesus and never return. Then I asked him to check it out and see if the pain was gone, so he would know that Jesus loved him and was inviting him into a personal relationship.

He shrugged his right shoulder and then his left. Then he did it again. Next, he stretched his arms above his head, and then he stood up and did something that looked vaguely like the chicken dance. His shoulders both seemed to be working perfectly, and I saw no sign of pain.

"On a scale of 1 to 10, with 10 being where you started, what is your pain level right now?"

"Well, I'd have to say, it's about . . ." he paused for effect, " . . . 1."

"It's at 1?" I asked.

He grinned, "I'm not about to give you the personal satisfaction of telling you it's at 0."

I could see from the huge smile on his face that 0 was exactly where it was.

"The pain is gone?" I asked.

"Seems to be."

I reached over, clasped his shoulder and told him, "Jesus healed you because He loves you and wants to have a relationship with you." I proceeded to explain God's plan of salvation.

For months after that, every time I went into his workplace and saw him, he would call out, "Hey, Robby, watch what I can do!" Then he would roll his arm around in a big circle, showing me that he was completely pain-free. "I haven't done that since I was in my teens."

Will You Pray for Me?

If you don't know whom to pray for, ask God to show you and He will. He may even bring them to you. Or just ask anyone how you can pray for him or her.

I have a friend named Chris who was doing his devotional one morning when God gave him a vision of a very specific beach area in Southern California. He saw a man running up the sandy hill from the beach, carrying a surfboard under his arm and with the upper part of his wet suit hanging from his waist. Chris then saw himself telling the man about Jesus and the guy giving his heart to Christ.

Chris knew the beach well because it wasn't far from his home, so he immediately went out, got into his car and drove there. As he parked and walked through the opening to a small cliff area connected to the beach, he saw a surfer finishing his wave. The guy then unzipped his suit to his waist and let it hang down, grabbing his board under his arm. Then he came running up the section of beach Chris had seen that morning in his prayer time. Everything was exactly the way he had seen it.

Now, all this was happening shortly after Chris read my book *Do What Jesus Did*. In that book, I told the story of a woman who felt that God had directed her to go into a convenience store and stand on her head in front of the clerk. What a silly thing to do, right? But after she did it, she discovered that the clerk had been praying, "God, if You're real, show me by having someone come in here and stand on their head."

Once the surfer reached the cliff area, he said hello to Chris. Chris greeted him back and asked if the surfing was good this morning.

"It's perfect," the guy replied.

They introduced themselves to each other and talked for a while. The surfer's language was a little bit rough, which gave Chris the impression that he wasn't a Christian. In fact, after hearing the way the guy talked, Chris concluded that bringing up Jesus after this would only embarrass him and make him feel awkward. Instead, he excused himself and headed back toward the parking area.

After he was about twenty feet away, the guy hollered out to him, "Hey, Chris, do you know anything about Jesus Christ that you can tell me?"

As you can imagine, Chris was in shock. "What did you say?"

"Well, I know this may sound crazy, but early this morning I had a dream that I was at this very area and a guy kind of like you walked up and told me about Jesus. Chris, I don't know anything about Jesus, but would really like to."

Chris proceeded to share the Gospel with the guy, prayed with him to accept Christ, and then got him plugged in at his church.

Don't Wait for Direction

I believe that Gods expects us to seek His direction and guidance in every area of life. But I don't believe we should wait for Him to give us the green light before we pray for someone. This is one area where we must be proactive and step out, expecting that God will show up.

Jesus told us to heal the sick. I don't see anywhere in the Scriptures where He says, "But don't pray for anyone unless I tell you to." It's true that Paul tells Timothy, "Do not be hasty in the laying on of hands" (1 Timothy 5:22), but it's clear from the context that he's talking about ordaining or commissioning someone for service in God's Kingdom.

When I was speaking at a conference once, a pastor came up to me and said, "I tell my church, don't you dare pray for someone until the Lord has told you to."

I said, "So you are training the members of your church to act like slaves! They are free in Christ. They need to know that they're free to do the things that Jesus did. Don't try to put them back into a slavery mentality."

If you need a directive before moving out in the power of God, you are stuck in a slavery mentality. If you move out in faith because there is a need to be met, then you have what I call an heir mentality.

So many times, it is in chance encounters that we see the power of God unleashed.

Some friends and I were at a shopping mall after a weekend training time in the United Kingdom when I saw a young man hobbling toward me on crutches. An attractive young woman I took to be his girlfriend was walking beside him, and I could see her concern for his well-being.

I called out to him, "What happened to your leg?"

"I destroyed my knee playing rugby," he said.

I got up, walked over to them and said, "It looks painful."

"It is. In fact, the doctor told me I'll never be able to play rugby again." He paused. "And I love rugby."

"Well, I'll tell you what. Jesus Christ can heal that leg right now if you let me pray for you."

"Of course."

I had no specific directive to pray for him, but I know what the power of Jesus can do.

As I often do with people, I told him to let me know how his pain level changed as I prayed for him, with 10 being the highest possible level and 0 being no pain.

"It's a 10 for sure," he replied.

I put my hand on his shoulder and prayed in the name of Jesus for the muscles and tendons to be healed and all pain to leave his leg by the authority of Christ. Then I asked him about the pain level.

Sounding shocked, he said, "It's much better! I'd say it's at a 2."

"Then let me pray for you again." I took authority over the injury in Jesus' name and again commanded it to be healed and the pain to leave.

"It's . . . gone."

"Are you sure? Don't be nice to me."

"Yes, I'm sure. Zero pain."

I told him to make sure, and he gingerly put his foot on the ground, which didn't make his girlfriend happy.

"No, don't do it!" she admonished him. "The doctor told you not to put any pressure on that leg for weeks."

"But there is no pain." He put his foot down harder. And then, much to his girlfriend's consternation, he handed me his crutches and began to walk around.

"Please be careful," she called out.

"I'm fine. The pain is gone."

"Are you sure?"

"I am!"

Obviously, he was telling the truth. His walk was completely normal. I couldn't detect a single sign of a limp.

When he thanked me, I told him, as I almost always do, "Jesus just invited you to a relationship with Him by healing your leg. How would you like to respond to Him?"

He said, "I need to consider that a bit."

A few minutes later, they walked off together, each happily carrying a crutch.

The Gift of Healing

People are always saying to me, "Robby, I would do what you do, but I don't have the gift of healing, as you do" (though I've never said that of myself). So, I want to close this chapter with an important question: Do you have the gift of healing? Although I do believe that God calls every Christian to pray for people who are sick and hurting, I also believe that some people have the supernatural gift of healing.

As the Bible says,

> To one there is given through the Spirit a message of wisdom, to another a message of knowledge by means of the same Spirit, to another faith by the same Spirit, to another gifts of healing by that one Spirit, to another miraculous powers, to another prophecy, to another distinguishing between spirits,

to another speaking in different kinds of tongues, and to still another the interpretation of tongues. All these are the work of one and the same Spirit, and he distributes them to each one, just as he determines.

1 Corinthians 12:7–11

I believe the apostles Peter and Paul both had the gift of healing. Acts 5:15 tells us that sick people were healed when Peter's shadow fell on them. And the nineteenth chapter of the same book says, "God did extraordinary miracles through Paul, so that even handkerchiefs and aprons that had touched him were taken to the sick, and their illnesses were cured and the evil spirits left them" (verses 11–12).

How can you tell if you have the supernatural gift of healing?

- ► Pray for others who are sick and in need.
- ► Ask God to show you if He has given you the gift of healing.
- ► Ask your pastor, mature Christian friends and others in spiritual authority if they believe the gift of healing is at work in you.

When I asked you if you have the gift of healing, you probably answered, "Who, me? Of course not."

But are you sure? The only way to find out for certain is to start praying for as many people as possible. Wouldn't it be sad to get to heaven someday and find out that you had always had the gift of healing, but had never used it? It would hurt to think that you could have prevented so much sickness, suffering and death, but never discovered that you had the power to do it.

And one thing I've always said is, if you don't have the supernatural gift of healing, try using the gift of obedience.

Jesus instructed all of us as His followers to heal the sick. He did not say, "And, let those of you who have the gift of healing pray for the sick. The rest of you can just tell them how bad you feel that they're going through such a rough time." No! He told us to heal the sick, period—end of story.

Healing in the Dominican Republic

Early this year, I traveled to the Dominican Republic for a Power and Love conference. A guy named Isa Cross wrote to tell me what happened when he heard all the testimonies from people who were healed or delivered from difficult situations:

> After one of your trainings with us, I wanted to have that authority to stand and pray for sick people, but I didn't have the courage, because I was more focused on "my fails" than on what God was going to do. . . . On the third day of the conference, you said something that really changed the way I see things: "If you don't have the gift of healing, try obedience."
>
> I said, "Okay, Lord, I'm gonna do what You told me to do in Matthew 10:7–8: 'As you go, preach this message: "The kingdom of heaven is near." Heal the sick, raise the dead, cleanse the lepers, drive out demons. Freely you have received; freely give'" [BSB].

Isa went on to say that when the time for outreach to the community came, strange things began to happen. People got healed. Demons were cast out. How did this happen? Isa says it came through obedience:

> I just obeyed every time the team members told me, "Okay, it's your time to pray." Now, every time I see sick people, I obey this command—and God hasn't failed me yet. Every time is a win-win situation with Jesus.

YOUR ACTIVATION GUIDE

- ▸ Whom are you praying for? Who else should be added to your list?
- ▸ I've always said the way to spell faith is *r-i-s-k*. What risks do you think God wants you to take for Him and His Kingdom?
- ▸ When was the last time you took a risk for God? What did you learn from the experience?
- ▸ What does this mean to you: "If you don't have the gift of healing, try obedience"?
- ▸ Do you think you have the gift of healing? Why or why not? If you're not sure, how can you find out?

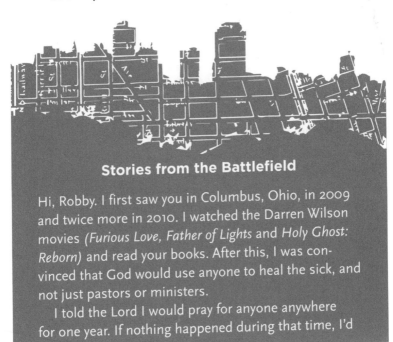

Stories from the Battlefield

Hi, Robby. I first saw you in Columbus, Ohio, in 2009 and twice more in 2010. I watched the Darren Wilson movies (*Furious Love, Father of Lights* and *Holy Ghost: Reborn*) and read your books. After this, I was convinced that God would use anyone to heal the sick, and not just pastors or ministers.

I told the Lord I would pray for anyone anywhere for one year. If nothing happened during that time, I'd know that it wasn't for me. Well, after four months of praying for many people, a friend of mine named Kevin tore up his knee while running. I prayed for it and the Lord healed Kevin's knee instantly. Since then, I have seen blind eyes open, short legs grow out, deaf ears open, people get up out of wheelchairs and walk, hundreds of backs healed. . . .

I support you and your family in prayer by name daily. I know your faith comes from your mother!

—Wendell Schultz

4

Speak His Words and Do His Works

Do not worry about how you will defend yourselves or what you will say, for the Holy Spirit will teach you at that time what you should say.

Luke 12:11–12

I recently read that when Americans are asked to name their greatest fear, public speaking takes the top spot. That surprises me a bit, considering the violence and turbulence that swirls all around us in these last days. Then again, I'm not among those who are terrified by speaking in front of an audience—unlike my wife, Angie—since I've been doing it my entire life.

But if the idea of public speaking makes you feel nervous—as it does most Americans—then imagine how you'd feel in this situation: You're standing on a stage in front of hundreds of people who are all looking at you expectantly, waiting for you to deliver a word from the Lord that will have a major impact on them and maybe even change their lives. And you don't have a single thing to say.

That's what happened to a young man named Jordan Wright.

And I'm the one who put him in that uncomfortable position. I wasn't playing a joke on him. I wanted to put him in a place where he had to trust God—because I knew God would come through.

I first met Jordan when he was nineteen. His parents were then pastoring the Trent Vineyard Church, the largest Vineyard congregation in the United Kingdom. They are now the national directors of the Vineyard Churches UK & Ireland.

I was in England, speaking at their church, and Jordan's mom, Debby, asked if I would spend a few minutes with Jordan in their garden. She told him that I had a strong prophetic gift, and she wanted me to prophesy over him. She assured him that she hadn't told me anything about him, which was true. I knew how old he was and that he was his parents' youngest child. That was it.

We sat down together, and I prayed that the Lord would give me a word for Jordan. As I began to pray, I saw a picture of a street roundabout with three exits. Most Americans would call it a traffic circle. I told Jordan what I'd seen and said, "It seems to me that you have three options in front of you. The Lord is saying that the one that seems most risky to you is the one He's really in."

I also told him that it would be a challenge, but that there was to be a spiritual awakening for him. "Does that make sense to you?" I asked.

Jordan nodded. "Yes, it's very interesting." He explained that he had three job offers and was trying to decide which one to take. He told me that the offer he really wanted to take was the riskiest one. What he didn't tell me was that his life was at a spiritual low point. Even though he considered himself a

Christian, he was barely going to church, hardly ever prayed or read his Bible, and just didn't have much of a spiritual life.

But he seemed to understand that God was talking to him. In fact, he was so impressed by the prophecy that had been given through me that he came to the service that evening with a young lady friend and asked if I would prophesy over her. The presence of the Holy Spirit was really powerful that night. People were shaking, falling to the floor and crying out when demons left them, as God made His presence known. "Party Time," as my son Micah calls it. Of course, I was happy to prophesy over Jordan's friend. I heard later that what the Lord had spoken through me was spot-on, and she gave her life to Christ before the service was over that night.

Shortly after that, Jordan took the job he wanted and moved to London. It wasn't very long before he was making a name for himself in real estate, selling multimillion-dollar properties, and pretty much living the good life. But not spiritually. Over the next couple of years, he would call me from time to time to catch me up on his life and ask me to pray for him.

A Flame Rekindled

Jordan moved into an apartment with a friend who didn't have much of an interest in spiritual things, and they started dabbling in drugs. But one night they got to talking about God, and his roommate told him that he had once been a strong believer in Christ. He particularly remembered a speaker he had heard who convinced him that God's love could and would overcome the powers of darkness.

The friend said, "I remember that he was speaking, and the electric power suddenly went off in the middle of the service. There were about six thousand people in there, and it was completely dark. The preacher said, 'We're going to pray and the lights will come back on. This will be a sign that we're involved in spiritual warfare.' And as soon as he prayed, the lights came back on."

Jordan asked, "Do you remember the speaker's name?"

"Yeah, John Wright."

"That's my father!"

As the two of them talked further about this, and as Jordan thought about the legacy of faith he had received from his mom and dad, he and his roommate rededicated their lives to Christ. They stopped experimenting with drugs, got back into a good church, and started spending time with the Lord. Shortly after that, Jordan quit his high-paying job because his employer wanted him to do some things that he considered unethical. The pressure came to a head one afternoon when Jordan decided that he had to choose between God's way and his company's way—and he wasn't about to go against God. Not again.

By this time, he had established an excellent track record in the real estate world. He was well-known in London and could have had his pick of a number of plum positions.

But I felt that God had something better in mind. I also felt that Jordan had something much better to offer God—and the world.

"I think you need to spend some time getting closer to God," I told him. "Why don't you come to the United States and get involved in ministry for three months or so? You can live with Angie and me, I can pay you a stipend, and you can travel with me."

The more he thought about it, the more he liked the idea, even though it meant giving up the big salary and simplifying his life. He was willing to put his career on hold to get closer to Christ.

We made plans for Jordan to come to the United States, and I booked a flight from London to Chicago. But the day before he was to come, he fell terribly ill. He was feverish, achy and had an intensely sore throat. He was so sick, in fact, that it took every ounce of his energy just to get out of bed. There was no way he was strong enough to make it to the airport and then endure an eight-hour flight. He called his mother to let her know what was going on, and she was so alarmed by the way he sounded that she called an ambulance to transport him to the hospital. Doctors there diagnosed him with mononucleosis.

A couple of days later, he called and told me that he was home and feeling somewhat better, although the sickness was not completely gone. He also felt he was dealing with spiritual warfare, and that if he came to Chicago despite the sickness, the Lord would make him well. But his mother, who is a woman of great faith, didn't exactly see it that way. Like any loving mom, she was worried about her son. She wanted him to stay put in London until his health and strength returned.

I told him, "Well, I'm certainly not going to tell you to go against your mother's wishes. You have to do whatever you believe the Lord is telling you to do."

He decided that God wanted him to come, so he called and booked a flight for the following day. But it seemed the devil had another trick up his sleeve. Jordan went to get his papers together, and his passport was nowhere to be found.

He looked everywhere he could think of, but there was no sign of it—and of course, he couldn't get on the plane without his passport. He finally called the passport office a few minutes before closing time, and he asked if they could rush him a copy of his passport by the following day. Now, if you've ever had to replace your passport, you know that doesn't happen overnight. It can be a long process—in England as well as the United States.

But by God's grace, Jordan got through to a caring person who agreed to go the extra mile to help. She punched up his information on her computer and said, "I can probably get it in the mail tonight. And that way, you should have it tomorrow."

The next day turned out to be a race against time. Jordan and his father went to their local post office and waited for the truck to come in with mail from central London. Somehow, they persuaded postal authorities to give them the letter as soon as it passed through the sorting process. From there, passport in hand, they rushed to the local station to catch a train to Heathrow Airport. There was not a moment to spare, and the stress was made worse by the fact that Jordan was still feeling horrible. He didn't want to admit it to his dad or himself, but his mono symptoms were flaring up. Even so, he still felt certain that he was doing what God wanted him to do.

Healed!

Again, by God's grace, Jordan got to the gate just as the plane was boarding. He said good-bye to his dad, made his way down the Jetway—and as soon as he set foot on the aircraft his mono symptoms completely disappeared. No more aches. No more feverish feeling. No more fatigue. In fact, energy filled his body. He felt completely fine and never had to take another bit of the medicine his doctor had prescribed.

The first weekend after Jordan arrived in Chicago, I had a conference at an Assembly of God church in Wisconsin. Because I hadn't been sure when Jordan was coming, I hadn't booked him a plane ticket. I wasn't even sure, what with all his dilemmas, that he would arrive in the United States. So I asked our college pastor, Tim, and another young man who was involved in college ministry, Jamie, if they would drive him to the conference and then spend the weekend with us there.

As they drove along and got to know each other better, Tim asked Jordan if he had ever been filled with the Holy Spirit and spoken in tongues.

Jordan replied that he had tried it once, and while he thought the experience was fine for other people, he told Tim, "It's just not for me."

Tim and Jamie both protested that tongues is a gift for everybody.

Jordan politely insisted that it wasn't something he was interested in pursuing. Case closed.

The next day was Saturday, the first day of the conference, and I was scheduled to speak on the subject of prophetic ministry. I said, "Before I speak on this, I want to give you a demonstration. Tim and Jamie, come up on the stage with me. And Jordan, you, too."

He shook his head and said, "No, I don't do this type of ministry."

I smiled and said, "Well, you do now. Come on up here."

He did as I asked, but very reluctantly. I could see by the look on his face that he was thinking, *What did I get myself into?*

I asked Tim to give a prophetic word for someone in the audience, which he did. Then I gave the microphone to Jamie, and he also gave a prophetic word. After that, I handed the mic to Jordan and told him it was his turn.

He shook his head, "I don't do this. I'm not even sure what you're talking about. I really . . ."

"Just pick someone out of the audience," I told him. "Say, 'The Lord wants you to know,' and then keep talking. The Lord will put the words in your mouth."

He stood there for a while, looking bewildered. Then he pointed at a couple sitting toward the back of the sanctuary. "I'm getting the word *truck* for you," he said. "And that's all I get. Just *truck*."

The man's mouth fell open.

"Does that mean anything to you?" Jordan asked.

The man stood up. "Yes, it does," he said. His voice broke with emotion as he explained, "My wife and I have a ministry to truckers. But we've been thinking that maybe God is calling us in a different direction."

His wife finished the story: "We were praying about it as we drove here this morning. We asked the Lord to have someone say the word *truck* to us if He wanted us to keep on doing what we're doing."

"God just used you to answer our prayer," her husband said.

An enthusiastic murmur swept through the congregation. As for Jordan, it seemed that giving his first prophetic word had flipped a switch into the *on* position. The gift that had always been inside him had been activated, and now he couldn't turn it off.

He turned toward a woman with a perfect, every-hair-in-place hairdo and a stylish blue suit.

"God says that you're a very strong woman and you struggle with the need to be in control."

Oh, no! I thought. *I've got to get the microphone away from him before he gets us all into trouble.*

I made another grab at it, but he kept on going: "You've been asking the Lord to help you with this, and He wants you to know that He's heard your prayers, and He will. . . ."

The lady burst into tears.

"Thank you!" she sobbed. "It's true. I know I come across as so hard-edged sometimes—and it's not who I want to be. I've been praying that the Lord would soften me, and help me be gentler and less opinionated. It means so much to know He understands."

I again tried to take the mic away from Jordan so we could continue with the service, but he was on a roll.

"And you," he said to a young man in the third row. "Somebody has been stealing from you. You're aware of it, but you're not really sure what to do about it. The Lord says He wants you to pray for the thief. If you do, He'll change the man's heart."

Once again, the gentleman heartily agreed with the word Jordan had given. "It's my neighbor," he said. "I've had a suspicion that he's been stealing from me for quite a while. I even confronted him about it, but he denied it."

He went on to say that he had been wondering if he should go to the police, or perhaps try to confront the man again. But now he had his answer—prayer, and God's mercy.

Holy Ghost Power at the Restaurant

I finally succeeded in getting Jordan to relinquish the microphone to me, and the service resumed. But he still wasn't done for the day. After the service, the pastor invited us all to a local restaurant for lunch. We ended up making quite a stir there as the Holy Spirit's power blew up the place.

The first person we encountered as we walked through the door was the hostess. After we gave her a name and the number of persons in our party, Jordan said, "The Lord tells me that you're worried about your son."

She stopped a minute, as if she'd been slapped in the face. Then a single tear trickled down her cheek. "Yes, I am. He's so . . ."

"Depressed," he finished her sentence.

"Yes. I've been feeling helpless about it. I just don't know how to help him."

"The Lord wants you to know that He's watching over your son, and He will bring him safely through this difficult time."

The woman dissolved into a torrent of grateful tears.

Then, after we were seated, Jordan suddenly pushed his chair back and nearly ran across the dining room to talk to a man sitting at a table with three young children.

"The Lord wants you to know that He appreciates what a good father you are. That's why He brought these kids into your life, even though you never had any children of your own."

More tears came as the man dabbed at his eyes with his handkerchief.

"I adopted these kids when I married my wife," he said. "I did that because their 'real' dad didn't want anything to do with them. But I couldn't love them any more than I do, even if they had been born to me."

"I know. And the Lord does, too."

When the waitress came to our table, Jordan told her that God had revealed to him that she was suffering from severe back pain, and he asked if he could pray for her. She agreed and was immediately healed.

Before we left the restaurant, Jordan had even spent a few minutes talking to the manager in private. When I asked him later what it was all about, he said the Lord had revealed to him that the man was involved in an inappropriate relationship with one of his employees. Apparently, when confronted about it, the fellow had admitted it. Jordan told him that he needed to give up the relationship, because it wasn't pleasing to God. If he would do that, the Lord would help him repair and strengthen his relationship with his wife. The two of them wound up praying together about the situation.

The whole day went like this. It was almost as if somebody had rubbed the magic lamp and let the genie out. Jordan reminded me of a baby learning to walk, one who starts off with a few shaky steps and then starts running all over the place, going so fast he's nearly impossible to catch. So much for "I don't do this type of ministry." I could see on his face that even he was flabbergasted by what the Lord was doing through him. He had this incredible gift inside him, but it had lain dormant all this time because he had never stepped out in faith to activate it.

I thought about all the people who had missed a special word of blessing, encouragement or warning from the Lord because Jordan had not utilized the gift the Lord had given him. And that is not meant to be an indictment against Jordan Wright, whom I saw aspire to be one of the godliest young men I've known while he lived with us. There are millions of Christians who could do tremendous good if they would only activate the gifts God has given them.

Think of the thousands and millions of people who have missed out on God's blessings because of our reluctance to act. They haven't received healing because we haven't activated and exercised our God-given ability and right to pray the prayer of faith and see them made whole. They haven't been willing to consider the claims of Jesus Christ because they haven't seen the Gospel confirmed with signs and wonders. They have made wrong decisions and drifted into sin because no one came forward to tell them, "The Lord wants you to know . . ."

As I watched my young friend in action, I was struck by an urgency to see people put their faith into action to minister the love of Jesus to the lost and suffering souls who live all around us. I was reminded of the apostle Paul's words to his young son in the faith, Timothy: "I remind you to fan into flame the gift of God, which is in you through the laying on of my hands. For the Spirit God gave us does not make us timid, but gives us power, love and self-discipline" (2 Timothy 1:6–7). The King James Version says to "stir up the gift." If Paul were writing to a tech-savvy, 21st-century audience, he very well might say, "Activate the gift that is in you."

Some people spend years waiting for God to do something He has already done. What we need to do is grab hold of what He's given us and use it the way He intended for us to.

As I said, once Jordan had activated the gift of prophetic ministry, there was no holding him back. At the conclusion of the evening service on Saturday, I asked him if he would step to the back of the auditorium and preside over the table where we were selling books, DVDs and other teaching materials.

He greeted the first man who reached the table with, "God wants to deliver you from your addiction to petty theft. He showed me that you've been stealing stuff like peanut butter."

The man couldn't deny it. His face turned red and his shoulders drooped a bit, but he wasn't about to try to lie to the Lord.

He said, "You know, I've been helping a shut-in, and for some reason I've been stealing his peanut butter. I don't know why. I just can't seem to help it."

Kind of trivial, huh? But more proof that God sees, knows and cares about everything!

Kingdom Rush

Sunday afternoon, after the final session of the weekend, Tim, Jamie and Jordan got in their car for the drive back to Illinois. As they set out on the interstate, Tim and Jamie again started talking about the power and release that came to them through praying in tongues. Just as before, Jordan was resistant. He was not unkind, but he insisted, as he had earlier, that speaking in tongues just wasn't for him. He also told them he was really tired and thought he'd take a nap. He settled down, put his head back and promptly began speaking in tongues.

The way Jordan remembers it, he had just put his head back when he felt someone grab his leg, as if to wake him up.

"What? What's going on?"

"Are you hearing that?"

"Hearing what? I don't hear anything."

"You've been speaking in tongues," Tim and Jamie told him.

"That's impossible," he protested. "I don't speak in tongues."

"That's what you've been doing for the last fifteen minutes," Tim laughed.

"That's right," Jamie agreed. "As soon as you put your head back, you started speaking in tongues."

"But I was just taking a nap."

Jordan grabbed his cell phone, pushed the button for the dictation app, and blurted out a few words in an unknown language. Shocked by what had just occurred, he checked to see how the phone had interpreted the words that had just come out of his mouth.

Here's what he read: "Kingdom Rush on a Sunday."

After we got back home, Jordan had those words tattooed on the inside of his forearm. He explained that he never wanted to forget what God had done for him on that weekend. It was an important turning point in his life.

Jamie had taken Jordan out to take part in some street evangelism the first night after he arrived in the States, and Jordan was intimidated by what he saw. He came back shaking his head and saying, "I don't think I can do this."

I admit, it can be difficult the first time you approach someone on the street and try to share God's love with him or her. And it can be especially difficult in some of the areas we go into, where there are many gangbangers, drug dealers, addicts and the like—people who are desperately in need of God's love, but who don't want to hear about it.

But after what happened to him during that following weekend in Wisconsin, Jordan loved going out on the streets to let people know about the peace, life and healing to be found in Jesus Christ. I saw many tough-looking characters dissolve into tears when they learned from Jordan that Jesus loved them, wanted a relationship with them, and had given His life in order that they might have forgiveness and eternal life.

The best news is that the same Spirit that transformed Jordan's life is also available to you, to me and to every believer.

White Noise from Heaven?

A lot of exciting things happened on that weekend trip to Wisconsin, but there were some silly moments, too. I want to take just a moment to tell you about one of those, because I think it will make you laugh—as it did all of us.

During the conference, Tim, Jamie and Jordan stayed in the home of a family who attended that Assembly of God. The two J's slept on couches in the basement, whereas Tim had a guest room all to himself. (I don't know why he was so fortunate. He must have drawn the shorter straw.)

Sometime late on Saturday evening, Jordan got up to go the bathroom. On his way there, he passed Tim's room and was shocked to hear an otherworldly sound emanating from inside.

He leaned closer to the door so he could hear it better. Yes! It was the sound of a mighty, rushing wind blowing through Tim's room!

Jordan had had some exciting experiences with the Spirit that day, so you can't really blame him for thinking of the second chapter of Acts, where the sound of a great wind announced the Holy Spirit's arrival on the Day of Pentecost. He dropped to his knees in the hallway and raised his arms in worship. The sound went on for ten or fifteen minutes, while Jordan continued to worship the Lord.

Then suddenly the door opened, and Tim stood there looking down at him.

"What are you doing?" Tim asked.

"There's a mighty, rushing wind blowing through your bedroom!"

"A mighty, rushing wind?" Tim sputtered. "What in the world are you . . . ? Oh, wait! That's my white noise app."

Seems it wasn't a heavenly sound after all. Just a little white noise from Tim's cell phone to help him fall asleep. As I said, we all had a good laugh about that one!

What the Bible Says about Prophecy

When they hear the word *prophecy*, most people picture someone like John the Baptist. They think of a wild-eyed man with a bushy head of hair that shoots out in every direction, living by himself in the wilderness, wearing clothes made of camel's hair, and subsisting on locusts and wild honey.

That may or may not be an accurate picture of a prophet—but it has almost nothing to do with the gift of prophecy we're talking about, which is available to all believers. Jesus said that His sheep listen to His voice (see John 10:27). When we hear His voice, we can prophesy in His name to comfort, strengthen and exhort believers. Here's some of what the apostle Paul had to say about the gift of prophecy:

> Follow the way of love and eagerly desire gifts of the Spirit, especially prophecy. For anyone who speaks in a tongue does not speak to people but to God. Indeed, no one understands them; they utter mysteries by the Spirit. But the one who prophesies speaks to people for their strengthening, encouraging and comfort. Anyone who speaks in a tongue edifies themselves, but the one who prophesies edifies the church. I would like every one of you to speak in tongues, but I would rather have you prophesy. The one who prophesies is greater than the one who speaks in tongues, unless someone interprets, so that the church may be edified. . . .
>
> For you can all prophesy in turn so that everyone may be instructed and encouraged.
>
> 1 Corinthians 14:1–5, 31

How does God speak to us? There are many ways. I want to look at some of them in more detail with you so you can recognize them.

1. He may speak in an audible voice.

When John baptized Jesus, a voice spoke from heaven and said, "This is my Son, whom I love; with him I am well pleased" (Matthew 3:17). Again, when Peter, James and John were on the Mount of Transfiguration with Jesus, God said: "This is my Son, whom I love; with him I am well pleased. Listen to him!" (Matthew 17:5). There are other instances in the Bible where God's voice was heard, and He still speaks today.

I know many people who have heard the audible voice of God. For most, it has been a one-time occurrence.

A woman who was going through a painful divorce heard Him say, "I am with you. Everything will be all right."

When I asked how she knew the voice belonged to God, she said, "I just knew."

In his book *Voice in the Night*, Pastor Surprise Sithole tells of the time when the voice of God woke him up in the middle of the night and said, "Surprise! Get out of the house. If you do not leave, you will die!"[1]

Hearing the audible voice of God is not a common occurrence. But it does happen, and when it does, it's not to be taken lightly.

2. He may speak in a still, small voice.

I love this passage from 1 Kings 19:11–13:

The LORD said, "Go out and stand on the mountain in the presence of the LORD, for the LORD is about to pass by."

Then a great and powerful wind tore the mountains apart and shattered the rocks before the LORD, but the LORD was not in the wind. After the wind there was an earthquake, but the LORD was not in the earthquake. After the earthquake came a fire, but the LORD was not in the fire. And after the fire came a gentle whisper. When Elijah heard it, he pulled his cloak over his face and went out and stood at the mouth of the cave.

The most frequent way God speaks to me, and, I believe, to most Christians, is through that still, small voice. Although He is the Creator of the universe, He doesn't always show up with thunder, flashes of lightning and hurricane-force winds—though I have known Him to do all that for me. He spoke the universe into existence, but He also whispers quiet messages into the hearts of men. Where did that longing in your soul come from? Did God put it there? How do you know? Did He really give you a specific message to deliver to that person over there? Or is your imagination just running away with you? The only way you can find out is by listening to God, more with your heart than with your ears, and learning to recognize His still, small voice.

I don't mean to imply that it takes practice to hear God's voice. He can speak to anyone, anywhere, anytime He chooses. But the problem is that the devil tries to impersonate Him. Paul says in 2 Corinthians 11:14–15 that Satan masquerades as an angel of light and his servants disguise themselves as servants of righteousness, so we always need to be on guard against them.

You can be on guard by knowing God's Word. Remember, something that goes against what the Bible teaches can't be from God. And if you're still not sure that what you were hearing came from God, run it past your pastor or some Christian friends whom you trust. The Bible says, "For lack of guidance a nation falls, but victory is won through many advisers" (Proverbs 11:14).

3. He speaks by popping words or Scriptures into our minds.

I've already told you about my friend Jordan Wright, who had the word *truck* pop into his mind. It didn't mean anything to him at the time, but it was a life-changing message for the couple who ran a ministry for truckers. I remember a friend telling me that when he first came to Christ, he often saw, in his mind's eye, a hand writing a Scripture verse on a chalkboard. When he looked up the verse, he discovered that it spoke directly to something he had been praying or asking about. For example, after he prayed about the end of the world, he saw "Matthew 24:35" written on that chalkboard: "Heaven and earth will pass away, but my words will never pass away." He wasn't greatly familiar with the Bible at that time, so he felt certain God was talking to him.

But be careful about this. There is an old joke about the man who was using the Bible to discern God's direction for his life. He opened it and read the first passage he saw: "And he cast down the pieces of silver in the temple, and departed, and went and hanged himself" (Matthew 27:5 KJV). Then he closed the Bible, opened it at random again and read, "Go, and do thou likewise" (Luke 10:37 KJV).

4. He speaks by popping pictures into our minds.

There have been many times during my ministry when God has spoken to me by flashing a picture, or a collage of pictures, into my mind. The old proverb says "a picture is worth a thousand words," and there are definitely times when that is true. Some things can become clear to us only when we see them, and that's especially true in our visually oriented age. In a single picture, we can see details that it might take a thousand words to explain.

If you are seeking God about something and a picture suddenly pops into your mind, don't get angry with yourself for letting your mind wander. It may be that God is speaking to you. The picture you see may not seem to have anything to do with what you were praying or thinking about, so when it comes, stop and ask God what He is saying to you.

I have had pictures come into my mind that made no sense to me. But when I shared them with the people I was praying for at the time, I discovered that they had great significance.

5. He speaks through dreams.

I think most of us have become kind of blasé about our dreams. We've come to believe that our dreams at night are nothing more than a jumbled-up repetition of what we've been through during the day. For instance, if you're on a road trip and you've been driving all day, you're just naturally going to dream that you're behind the wheel. Right?

Not necessarily. While we've all experienced dreams that seem to be little more than a pastiche of past experiences, I also believe there are spiritual dreams that come directly from the heart of God. The Bible is full of references to such dreams. Remember how angry Joseph's brothers were when they heard of his dream in which the sun, moon and stars bowed down to his star? Pharaoh's dream of the seven fat cows being devoured by seven skinny cows meant that famine was about to grip the Middle East. Daniel correctly interpreted a dream that deeply troubled King Nebuchadnez-zar of Babylon. (And not only interpreted it correctly, but told the king what the dream had been.) And, in the New Testament, Joseph had a dream warning him to take Jesus and Mary and flee into Egypt, and the Magi were warned in a dream not to share with Herod where the Messiah had been born.

If God used dreams in Bible times, He certainly can and does use them now. Joel spoke of the importance of dreams when he prophesied, "And it shall come to pass afterward, that I will pour out my spirit upon all flesh; your sons and your daughters shall prophesy, your old men shall dream dreams" (Joel 2:28 KJV). When I lie down to sleep at night, I often pray, *Lord, speak to me in my night visions* (as the prophet Daniel called them). And He does. As I wrote in *Do What Jesus Did*, "I've told so many spouses whose partners are not Christian to pray over their partners' pillows. I've heard story after story of how God has worked through that and brought dreams to the spouses that they couldn't ignore."[2]

6. He speaks by giving us sympathy pains or sensations.

Perhaps you have heard me or another evangelist suddenly say during a meeting, "There is someone here with a burning sensation at the top of the shoulder. If that's you, please come up here and let me pray for you."

How do I know that about a person? Often, it's because God has showed me by giving me a pain or sensation at the top of my shoulder. I've learned that this is a message to me that someone else is experiencing the same thing and God wants me to pray for that person.

Yes, it sometimes hurts to hear from God. But it's always worth it. I've had terrible headaches, excruciating back pain, stabbing pain in my knees—I could go on and on. Name it and I've probably had it. The difference is that I've had it momentarily because God is showing me what someone else is going through. Unless they get healed, they're going to keep on enduring that pain. Honestly, I doubt that the pain I experience is anywhere near as bad as what the real sufferers are dealing with. But it's enough to get my attention, and it certainly increases my desire to see people healed.

7. He sometimes speaks through others.

This can be one of the most important ways God speaks to us, but it can also be one of the most difficult ways to hear or discern His voice.

When I say that God speaks through others, I am mostly thinking of our spiritual leaders or others. But He can speak through anyone and everyone. God has spoken very directly to me through my four-year-old son, Caspian, even though he was unaware of it. The Bible book of Numbers even tells us that God used a donkey to speak to a man named Baalam.

I'm not saying that you should accept everything everybody says to you. But neither should you dismiss it out of hand without even considering it.

8. He speaks through the Spirit bearing witness.

Have you ever been reading the Bible when you came across a Scripture that seemed to jump right off the page at you? It might have been one you had read dozens of times before and never even thought much about. But all of a sudden, it seemed as though it were written in neon type. When that happens, it's the Holy Spirit bearing witness that this is a message to you straight from the heart of God.

The same thing may happen when you're listening to a song on the radio, conversing with a friend, or even driving down the street. Suddenly, a phrase, a picture on a billboard, or just about anything else grabs hold of you, and you know God is speaking to you. Your heart may start pounding, or your friend suddenly may sound as if he's speaking in an echo chamber, or you feel emotion rising up in you for no apparent reason at all. All of these things happen because you are standing in the presence of God and He is speaking to you.

In the book of Romans, Paul talks about the Spirit bearing witness: "The Spirit himself testifies with our spirit that we are God's children," and, "I speak the truth in Christ—I am not lying, my conscience confirms it through the Holy Spirit" (Romans 8:16; 9:1).

After pondering these eight ways that God speaks to us, you should consider which of these ways have been the pattern for how you have experienced God speaking to you. Which ones stand out as the ways you have heard His voice? Also, you may want to pray and ask the Father to speak to you through some of the other ways that you haven't experienced yet, so you can move on into the arena of greater things. An adventure awaits us there!

YOUR ACTIVATION GUIDE

- ▶ Have you ever had to choose between God and the world? If so, how did you choose? What happened?
- ▶ Are you facing a choice between God and the world right now? How can you ensure that you make the right decision?
- ▶ How much time do you spend in prayer listening to God? In your prayer time this week, practice talking less and listening more.
- ▶ What do you think Paul meant when he told Timothy to "fan into flame" the gift that was inside him? How can you fan into flame the gift or gifts the Lord has given you?
- ▶ Take a few minutes to listen for God's voice. What is He saying to you right now?

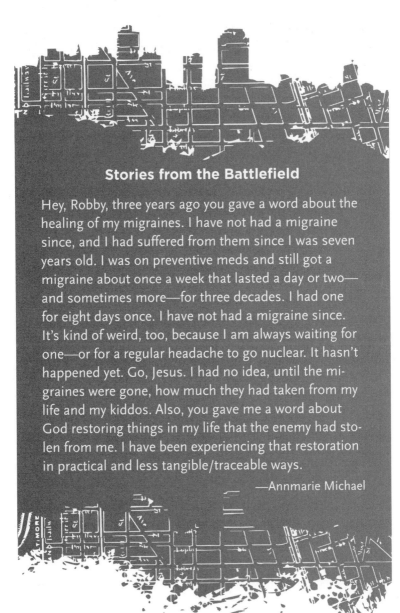

Stories from the Battlefield

Hey, Robby, three years ago you gave a word about the healing of my migraines. I have not had a migraine since, and I had suffered from them since I was seven years old. I was on preventive meds and still got a migraine about once a week that lasted a day or two—and sometimes more—for three decades. I had one for eight days once. I have not had a migraine since. It's kind of weird, too, because I am always waiting for one—or for a regular headache to go nuclear. It hasn't happened yet. Go, Jesus. I had no idea, until the migraines were gone, how much they had taken from my life and my kiddos. Also, you gave me a word about God restoring things in my life that the enemy had stolen from me. I have been experiencing that restoration in practical and less tangible/traceable ways.

—Annmarie Michael

5

Raise the Dead

Heal the sick, *raise the dead*, cleanse those who have leprosy, drive out demons. Freely you have received; freely give.

Matthew 10:8, emphasis added

The date was March 9, 2015. The place was a small village church in Inglewhite, England.

I had been invited to come there by the pastor of a conservative church because he wanted to learn more about healing as a means of bringing people to Christ. We were in the middle of an evening service in the church, with about two hundred people in attendance, when it happened.

It was an ordinary evening until a woman suddenly shouted, "My son! My son! He's having another stroke! Someone call an ambulance!"

Clearly, the young man sitting next to her was in distress. He had arched back in his seat, and his arms seemed to be contracting, drawing his hands up toward his face. He was stiff and twitching; it seemed that every muscle in his body was tight and tense.

I discerned a demonic presence over him and felt immediately that the spirit of death was present and trying to kill him.

Along with the pastor and several other members of the congregation, I rushed over to help. Gasping through her tears, his mother told us that her son Matt, who seemed to be in his late thirties, had suffered a stroke about a year earlier. She then looked directly at me and asked, "Can you help him?"

I put my hands on his chest and forehead and began to bind demonic power and command his body to be loosed in Jesus' name.

As I was doing this, I asked his mom if Matt was having an epileptic seizure. She said no, he had never had a seizure before.

Though emergency services had been called, we in the church were on our own, and the situation seemed desperate. I knew there was no time to waste. The young man's breath was coming in short, irregular gasps, and his skin was turning very red, then frighteningly purple. Several of us laid him out on the floor to give him more room, and I commanded Satan to leave him alone. Still, the spirit of death hovered around us like an evil fog, and I sensed it would not willingly loosen its grip on the young man.

Matt's breathing became more labored, his lips turned a darker shade of blue-black, and his mother cried out, "He's dying! My poor boy is dying!"

I had my hand on Matt's chest and assured his mother that his heart was still beating—although I could feel it getting weaker. As I continued to pray and fight for his life, it seemed that his every breath was more of a struggle than the last. (I discovered later that this is called "agonal breathing" and is the death rattle that happens when someone is dying and his or her body is shutting down.)

Then it happened. One more agonizing breath, then nothing . . . nothing. Matt stopped breathing. His head fell limply to the side, saliva poured out of his mouth, and his pupils became fixed and dilated.

"He's dead!" someone said.

"No, no!" It was Matt's mother.

A gentleman came and leaned over Matt. He shook his head. "I'm sorry; he's gone." The man revealed himself as a doctor.

Was the battle really over? Had death won again? My heart sank. I could see in my mind the faces of the thirty or so people whom I had prayed for so forcefully to be raised from the dead who never again opened their eyes. My prayers hadn't worked for them. Why should I expect them to work for Matt?

That's right, a voice in my head said. *You don't have the power; you never did.*

Then it hit me. Satan was afraid of what was coming next. Satan was projecting his fear over what was about to happen to get me to back off.

I felt my anger rise. "Sorry, little Luci," I said, using my name for Satan, "I'm not going to quit. I'm not going to walk away from Matt."

"You can't have him!" I said, and I began declaring the resurrection life of Jesus Christ over Matt. "You foul spirit of death, release him. Resurrection life of Christ, fill him now."

Matt suddenly gasped loudly, "Uhhhhhhh. . . ." He took one deep breath, and then another. Color began to return to his face. His eyelids fluttered and his breathing became more regular. His lips, which had been a deep blue, began to revert to their normal color.

He rolled himself onto his stomach. His breathing seemed normal now, and he began to push himself up.

"Take it slow," I said as he stood to his feet. "How are you feeling?"

His mother, her voice trembling, said, "I'm sorry. He can't speak since his stroke."

But he did speak, and he began answering my questions in complete sentences.

"He can speak!" his mother shouted in surprise.

He said, "What do you mean? Of course I can speak. But what's going on? What is everyone looking at?"

I turned him toward me, embraced him and declared a full impartation of life. I did this because I have a friend who had been brought back from the dead, and he had told me, "There is something about the chest-to-chest connection that seems to impart life." Then Matt hugged me again. He must have felt it, too.

A few minutes later, the ambulance arrived to transport him to the nearest hospital. The next day, the pastor and I went to see him. He seemed fine, except that he had torn his rotator cuff during the episode—so badly, in fact, that it would require surgery to repair it.

We chatted for a minute, and I asked him if he knew what had happened the night before.

"Whatever it was, it was pretty bad," he answered.

I told him he had died, and Jesus had brought him back to life through prayer.

Although some people not present that night refuse to accept what eighty of us remaining in the sanctuary did witness, this testimony has been read and believed by millions. In addition, I am gratified to have received many letters and emails from those who were motivated by it and went out and pursued raising the dead.

Jesus Meant What He Said

Jesus told His followers to raise the dead. I believe He meant exactly what He said. And He wouldn't have said it if it weren't possible.

How many people can you think of who have been raised from the dead? There is Jesus, of course. Then Lazarus, the brother of Mary and Martha. Jesus Himself raised at least two more people—the daughter of a synagogue leader named Jairus, and a young man known only as the son of a widow who lived in the town of Nain.

Peter raised a woman named Dorcas, a person of faith who was much beloved in her community because of all she did to help the poor. And then there was Paul raising a young man named Eutychus, one of my favorite Bible stories. Eutychus, as you may remember, fell asleep during an obviously long sermon Paul preached, and he fell backward out of a third-story window. The Bible says,

> Paul went down, threw himself on the young man and put his arms around him. "Don't be alarmed," he said. "He's alive!" Then he went upstairs again and broke bread and ate. After talking until daylight, he left. The people took the young man home alive and were greatly comforted.
>
> Acts 20:7–12

If you're keeping track, that's six. And there are three more in the Old Testament. The seventeenth chapter of 1 Kings tells of a widow's son whom the prophet Elijah raised from death, and the fourth chapter of 2 Kings tells how Elijah's successor, Elisha, also brought a little boy back to life.

Elisha was also involved in another resurrection. Second Kings 13:21 says, "Once while some Israelites were burying a man, suddenly they saw a band of raiders; so they threw the man's body into Elisha's tomb. When the body touched Elisha's bones, the man came to life and stood up on his feet."

That makes nine, and don't forget all those who came out of their tombs and went into the city after Christ's resurrection (see Matthew 27:52–53). I admit that it's still a very small fraction of all the people who have ever lived. But it also shows that it is not impossible to bring the dead back to life, no matter what medical science may say.

Besides, I have a feeling that Jesus raised many others whom the Bible doesn't tell us about. Remember what John says at the end of his gospel? "Jesus did many other things as well. If every one of them were written down, I suppose that even the whole world would not have room for the books that would be written" (John 21:25).

And just in case you're tempted to think that no one has been raised from the dead since the days of the apostles, let me say that I believe it happens more often than most of us realize. As I've already told you, I've seen it for myself. I have a written medical report confirming that it has happened from a doctor who was an eyewitness.

They Came Back from Beyond

There are many other examples of people being raised from the dead. The great evangelist Smith Wigglesworth is said to have raised fourteen people from the dead during the early years of the twentieth century. One of these was a woman who reportedly died when Wigglesworth and a friend were visiting with her in the hospital. She stopped breathing and had no pulse. Wigglesworth and his friend took the woman out of her bed and stood her body up against a wardrobe. Then he said, "In the name of Jesus, I rebuke this death," and her body began to tremble. He then commanded her to walk in the name of Jesus, which she did—back to her bed.

It is reported that when the woman was later questioned about what had happened to her, she said that she had been in heaven when Jesus pointed for her to leave, and she heard a voice telling her to walk in the name of Jesus.

The Spirit of Death in Sierra Leone

In April 2017 I had the privilege of traveling to Sierra Leone, in western Africa. This was the same trip I told you about in chapter 2, where we wound up sharing the love of Jesus in a village mosque. Sierra Leone is a beautiful country known for its white, sandy beaches. But it is a country that has been devastated by war, Ebola and unthinkable poverty.

Our goal for the trip, as always, was to train people in ministry and then take them out into the villages to do the things that Jesus did, "and even greater things than these."

In one of those villages, we encountered a man who was extremely ill with sickle cell anemia. The village had a clinic, but the clinic had no beds, so he lay on the floor. I've discovered that such things are not rare in the poorest rural areas of sub-Saharan Africa. The man lay there with a number of IV tubes attached to his arm. He had been there several days, lying flat on his back, too weak even to turn onto his side.

His body was racked with pain, the worst of it in his feet. One of the women in our group sought me ought and asked me to pray for him. She had gone out after my training and had found this man and prayed for him, but then she asked me to come back and pray, too. She told me, "He was complaining about his feet, so I prayed for them and God healed him. But now he says the pain is everywhere but in his feet."

I went back to the clinic with her, and I prayed for a complete healing. Suddenly, he leaped to his feet. He got up so fast he had to grab his knees to brace himself. Then he yanked the IV tubes out of his arm. I was afraid blood would come shooting out of those veins, but it didn't. He said that a sudden surge of energy had passed through his entire body. He felt great and was completely free from pain. The only things that hurt were his ankles, probably because he had jumped up so suddenly. After we prayed for his ankles, he said he felt perfectly fine, and he began walking around smiling because he felt so good.

While we were rejoicing over this victory, one of our team members, a major in the Sierra Leone army, came to give us some bad news. He had just received word that the wife of his commanding officer had died suddenly that morning. She had not been sick. Everything seemed fine. All of a sudden, she complained that her stomach was hurting, and then she collapsed and died.

Two thoughts came to me immediately: *1) It could be Ebola; 2) We've got to pray for this woman!*

Before we went into Sierra Leone, word was that the Ebola crisis was over. Still, we had been told to be extremely careful. Ebola is deadly, and prevention is the only cure.

When I said that we needed to pray for this woman, the major shook his head. "She's dead," he said, indicating that he felt it was too late for prayer.

"God can raise her up," I replied. "Do you know where the body is?"

"She's been transported to the morgue."

"Can you take us there?"

"Of course."

My friend Boris Eichelberger (one of the most empowering, courageous and wise missions leaders I've ever met) and I hopped into the major's car, and we headed for the morgue at the hospital, about two hours away.

We had gone about halfway, when we suddenly saw a police checkpoint up ahead. These checkpoints may suddenly spring up anywhere in Sierra Leone. You're driving along and you see a rope stretched across the road in front of you. There's no warning, like a sign that says, "Police checkpoint ahead." Just a couple of men standing on each side of the road, holding a rope stretched across the path.

It can be unsettling because you don't know why they're stopping you—and they can be heavily armed.

In this instance, they also seemed extremely angry. As soon as our driver stepped out of the car, the police captain was all over him, shouting and pointing. The only thing I could understand was the word *abado*, which he used several times. I heard this word often in Sierra Leone and came to understand that it means "white man."

Boris told me he thought it would be best if we sat quietly and didn't try to say anything, so he and I remained in the car, praying in the Spirit. The only thing I could think of was that we had had a confrontation with a self-proclaimed witch doctor earlier that morning. He was a powerful man in his village and did not want us there, talking about Jesus. Had he called ahead and asked the police to stop us?

We never found out, but God heard our prayers. After ten or fifteen minutes the police finally let us go, telling the major, "Take your white men and go."

We made it the rest of the way to the morgue without incident, although when we got there, we were denied entrance. Boris was persistent and unyielding. This touched the major. We were told that everything was locked up, and no key was available.

But as we were leaving, we saw a couple of men bringing in a body on a stretcher, so we followed them inside. There, we saw the body of the commander's wife lying on a slab. To be honest, we could already smell death.

Boris and I knew we were taking a risk because of the possibility that Ebola had caused this woman's death, but we put our hands on her shoulder, arms and head as we prayed for her to come back. We prayed fervently for about fifteen minutes. At the end of that time, I felt that we had done all we could do. I had heard that she was a devout Christian, so I knew that would make it harder to bring her back. Why would she want to leave the presence of Jesus, unless He told her to return to her body?

The whole time we were praying, both Boris and I had felt an extreme heaviness. There was a darkness in this place that was so thick you could almost reach out and touch it. I knew we were sensing the spirit of death.

The next day at our worship service, I felt the same dark presence. It seemed to surround a girl who was helping lead worship. When I asked someone to tell me about her, he replied that she was suffering from a severe chronic illness and had recently come out of a prolonged coma. Since then, she had been morose and lethargic, not at all the same happy girl she had once been. I saw that she also had a slight physical deformity. Nevertheless, God showed me a picture of her playing the piano.

"Actually, she's very musical," I was told. "She'd love to play the piano, but she can't because of her deformity."

"And what caused that?" I asked.

"An infection."

I also found out that she was about to see some specialists. Her mother was anxious to find out why the girl had gone into a coma, since her illness seemed under control. But I recognized the spirit of death, and I knew that she was under attack. After the service, I told her I wanted to pray for her, and she said she would be delighted.

As I prayed for her, I rebuked the spirit of death in Jesus' name. Her eyes rolled back in her head, and she began to sway back and forth as the spirit of death was broken off her.

Within an hour, this girl was bouncing around like a "normal" teenager, laughing, dancing and singing. People were amazed, asking things like "Wow! What happened to you?"

The difference was startling. The effects of her illness began to recede daily, and she was starting to get some mobility around the area of her deformity.

I believe this all happened because of being able to identify the spirit of death and deal with it in the name of Jesus. Had I not been to the mortuary the day before, I may not have been as sensitive to the young lady's need to be delivered from this spiritual attack. God used our willingness to pray for the dead to save a young girl's life!

A Final Word

I feel the need to make a few more points about praying for the dead. One point is that when we pray for a believer to be resurrected, our motive is not just for the person, but also for those he or she may be leaving behind. We pray because a husband would struggle to live without his wife and sweetheart. Because a mother's heart would be broken beyond repair if she lost her child. We pray because children need their mommy or daddy.

I know of many instances where believers died, went to heaven and then were told, "It's not your time yet. You have to go back to earth." I have not heard of a single instance when the person who came back to life has said, "I was so happy when I was told to go back into my body." Instead, everyone was disappointed, because they wanted to stay in heaven. For the believer, death is not a final defeat, but rather, a final victory. I wonder if this might not be one of the reasons Jesus cried before He raised Lazarus from the dead. Did it break His heart to know that He was calling his friend out of paradise and back into this world of heartache and woe?

My point is that we shouldn't feel defeated if we pray for someone who is saved and the person is not raised. We can instead rejoice for that person because he or she has graduated from life on this earth.

In the opposite case, we really need to be urgent about praying for the dead when the object of our prayers is passing into eternity without Christ. Your prayers may bring someone back and give that person a second chance to respond to the Gospel—and escape everlasting punishment in hell.

Another point I want to make has to do with a difficult question I've often been asked: Is it okay to attempt to raise the dead every time we have the opportunity? Or should we ask God for His will in each case? In other words, do we need a divine directive to pray for someone's resurrection?

My friend Todd White was asked one time at a conference that we were doing together if we should pray for everyone, or only for the ones God wants to heal. Todd stated, "God wants to heal everyone!" When someone objected on the grounds that not everyone we pray for is healed, Todd replied, "Show me the person Jesus didn't die for, and that's the one I won't pray for."

I am with Todd on this. My advice in the matter is to go for it, unless God tells you specifically and clearly not to pray for someone.

Let me add, however, that I am not advocating that anyone should spend all his or her time praying for the dead. I'm not instructing you to hang out in mortuaries and pray for the dead as they are brought in. Nor am I telling you to make a habit of attending funerals to pray for the dead there. (Although I should also add that neither am I discouraging you from doing any of these.)

But if you should see someone suddenly fall dead of a heart attack, by all means pray for God to raise the person.

If you come upon a car crash where someone has been killed, pray for restoration of life.

If, God forbid, a toddler in your neighborhood has been pulled from a swimming pool and is not breathing, pray for God to restore the breath of life.

It's important to know CPR and other lifesaving first aid. But it's even more important to be ready, willing and able to pray in the powerful name of Jesus, the One who has swallowed up death in victory!

YOUR ACTIVATION GUIDE

- ▶ Jesus told His disciples to go out and raise the dead in His name. Do you believe this command includes you? Why or why not?
- ▶ What did Jesus mean when He said to raise the dead? Are we to look actively for opportunities to pray for the dead, or just be ready when the situation arises? How does your answer affect your actions?
- ▶ What are some situations where you might be called on to raise the dead in the name of Jesus?
- ▶ Take some time to read again about the resurrection of Lazarus in the eleventh chapter of John. Why do you think Jesus waited so long to go to Lazarus? What lessons can we learn from this passage of Scripture?
- ▶ The Bible says that when Jesus went in to raise Jairus' daughter from the dead, "they laughed at him" (Mark 5:40). The King James Version says that "they laughed him to scorn." Are you willing to be laughed at for Jesus' sake? If not, ask Him to give you strength.

6

Salvation Has Come

For I am not ashamed of the gospel, because it is the power of God that brings salvation to everyone who believes: first to the Jew, then to the Gentile.

Romans 1:16

There is something even more exciting than healing the sick and raising the dead, and that is rescuing people from hell so they can live with Jesus for all eternity. Salvation is, after all, the primary purpose of signs and wonders. (The second reason is that God's heart is full of compassion for people who are hurting.) Let me tell you about my friend Mohamed.

I first met Mohamed in the gym where I go to work out. He was a fairly dark-skinned guy with a thick, black beard and a short, clean haircut. He looked to be of Arab descent. Whereas most of the people seemed to work out in groups or pairs, he was always by himself. I never heard anybody put him down or harass him in any way—but it was easy to see that some people were wary of him simply because he appeared Muslim. I love ministering to Muslims, and this one needed a friend. More than that, he needed Jesus.

I shifted my workout to match his, so on the same days we were working on the same body parts—shoulder day first, chest day next, and so on. My number one priority is always to tell people about Jesus, and I do whatever I can to make that happen. After about three weeks of seeing Mohamed every day, I finally introduced myself to him. I extended my hand and told him my name was Robby.

I wasn't surprised when he responded, "I'm Mohamed."

We shook hands and I told him, "I noticed that you and I seem to be working on the same parts of our bodies. How would you feel about working out together? That way, we could spot each other and help each other out."

He thought it was a good idea, so we agreed to meet at the gym five days a week. Two or three weeks went by, and we slowly got to know each other. Mohamed explained that he worked selling software for a computer company. He liked the technical part of his job, but sales were the big component.

In all that time, we had never talked about Jesus, though I had told him I pastored a church in town. It's fairly unusual for me to hold back, but I had a feeling that Jesus wanted me to wait until the time was right with Mohamed.

Then one day, I could tell that Mohamed's spirits were dragging. When I asked him what was wrong, he told me that he was struggling to meet his sales quota. He was afraid that if things didn't pick up, he was going to lose his job.

For the first time, I told him that I loved to pray for people. I offered to pray for him.

He thought about it for a moment or two and then declined my offer. "I know you'd pray to Isa [Jesus], and I'm a Muslim," he said.

We talked a little more about it, but he insisted that as a "good" Muslim, he could not agree to have a Christian pray for him. Of course, this disappointed me. But I wasn't going to let one setback stop me from trying to reach him for Jesus. I knew that if I persevered in the relationship, God would provide other opportunities to tell Mohamed about Jesus.

The next opportunity came a couple of weeks later, but not in a good way. Mohamed showed up at the gym looking like he'd lost every friend he ever had. I assumed it had something to do with his job.

"What's up?" I asked him. "Trouble with sales again?"

"No," he croaked, and his eyes filled with tears. "It's my sister."

He explained that his sister had just been diagnosed with stage 4 breast cancer. The tumor in her breast was roughly the size of a baseball, and it had penetrated into her chest wall. Her doctor told her that she had five months to live, maybe less.

Mohamed wiped his eyes on his shirt. "I don't know what I'm going to do. I've never lost anybody before. It really hurts!"

"Will you let me pray for her?" I asked.

He shook his head, "I don't know. . . ."

"If you allow me to come pray for her, Jesus will heal her."

"How can you say that?"

"I just know," I said. "Trust me . . . and trust Him."

Now, I had not received a word from the Lord that Mohamed's sister would be healed. Nor was I waiting for a word from the Lord. He says in the Bible that God will answer the prayer of faith offered up in His name. In other words, we've already been given a word, and we don't need another one. Yes, God may tell you specifically to pray for someone. He certainly does that with me. But that doesn't mean that you have to wait for a specific word before stepping out in faith. If you see a need, be willing to step out in faith and meet that need.

Anyway, Mohamed still hesitated, so I reminded him that Jesus is spoken of and honored in the Qur'an.

Finally, he agreed with me and invited me to come home with him and pray for his sister.

She was a sweet young lady, much too young to be dying from an insidious disease like breast cancer. I couldn't help but think of my mother, who had fought—and lost—her own battle with colon cancer. Then again, my mom had lived a good life of godly service, and the Lord had told me that He was going to take her home. This young lady had almost her entire life ahead of her.

As I prayed for her that day, I saw a picture in my mind of the tumor shrinking down to the size of a pea and then disappearing. When I asked the young lady if she was feeling anything, she said no, so I told her and her brother what the Lord had shown me. Still, nothing happened that we could see. There were no fireworks or voices or any other supernatural manifestations. There was nothing but faith on my part, and utter desperation on the part of Mohamed and his sister. Before I left, she told me that she was about to go in for another scan of the tumor, and she would let me know what the doctors told her.

I didn't hear anything for several days. Every time I saw Mohamed, he told me that his sister was "doing about the same." She hadn't yet been in for the scan, but there was no sign that God had answered my prayer. I wasn't discouraged, though. I was expectant.

Then one day it happened. He showed up at a small gathering at a restaurant for my birthday.

"Have you heard?" he asked.

"Heard what?

"My sister!" he shouted.

"What about her?" I asked, although I suspected what the answer would be.

"She finally got the scan. And when the doctor looked at it, he said the tumor had shrunk down to the size of a pea! He thought there must be some kind of mix-up or something, so he sent her to get an ultrasound, and then another scan, and when it came back . . ."

"The tumor was gone," I finished his sentence for him.

"Completely gone!" he shouted. "She's cancer-free!"

I threw my arms around him. "That's wonderful news! I knew Jesus would heal her."

"Yes, I guess He did, didn't He?"

Once again, God had confirmed the Gospel through signs and wonders. He responded exactly the way I had asked, first shrinking her tumor down to the size of a pea, and then making it disappear. The first step was totally unnecessary. He could have made the cancer disappear immediately, but if that had happened, people could have said that she had experienced a spontaneous remission or a misdiagnosis. But because He brought about the healing in stages, just as I had said He would, His power was clearly seen.

And the story doesn't end there.

Mohamed had more to tell me.

"Ever since I've been working out with you, my sales have shot through the roof."

Although he had refused my offer for prayer in this matter, his sales had gone up dramatically, and he felt strongly that it had happened because he was spending time with me.

"What do you think about all this?" I asked him.

He sighed deeply. "I don't know what to think of it. It has really blown my mind. You know, the Qur'an says that the ability to work miracles is the sign of a prophet."

As we continued talking, I reminded him that the Qur'an also instructs Muslims to study the teachings of Jesus.

"That's true," he admitted, "but I've never done that."

"Well, I have an idea," I said. "How about if we start a study group? We can set up some times for me to meet with your family, and we'll study His teachings together."

He loved the idea! "We'll have dinner together," he said. "We'll have lamb and hummus. . . ."

Mohamed couldn't wait to get started, but he had one caveat. He was willing to study the four gospels because they contain the teachings of Jesus. "But I don't want to study any of the other New Testament books."

"That's fine," I agreed. "We'll stick to the teachings of Jesus."

As it turned out, I was only able to meet with Mohamed and his family a couple of times before my travel schedule took off and I was on the road for much of the next several months. When it became apparent that I wasn't able to continue with the study, a friend of mine took over and continued to meet with the family every week.

And apparently, once Mohamed had studied the gospels, he decided that perhaps he did want to read some of those other New Testament books. I got a call from him a few months after we had started meeting together, and the minute I heard his voice, I could sense that he was beside himself with excitement.

"Robby," he asked, "have you ever read the book of Acts?"

"Oh, yes, many times."

"It's amazing! Isa does it, and then in the book of Acts the apostles do it!" He paused a moment and then said, "I think I'm going to read Romans next."

That was three or four years ago. Since then, Mohamed has read the entire Bible through at least twice. He now goes to church, prays in the name of Jesus, and carries the Bible with him instead of the Qur'an. He still goes to the mosque for afternoon prayers on Friday, and when there's someone in the congregation who needs healing prayer, the imam sends them to Mohamed!

The Best Thing Ever

What do you suppose Mohamed would say if you asked him to tell you the best thing that ever happened to him? Would he say it was seeing his sister healed from deadly cancer? No, although that is certainly something he will always remember with joy. Would he say that the best thing that ever happened to him was becoming someone who sees the power of God unleashed when he prays for others? No, although that, too, is an amazing, wonderful thing.

The best thing that has ever happened to Mohamed is the best thing that can happen to anyone. It's the best thing that has ever happened to me. It's the best thing that has ever happened to my wife, Angie. And to our six sons. Nobody I've ever met has ever had anything better happen to them than this: coming to know Jesus Christ as Lord and Savior, and obtaining eternal salvation through faith in Him.

This is the apex of everything we are talking about in this book. All signs and wonders are pointing toward God's offer of eternal, abundant life through Christ.

I don't know if this ever happens to you, but every once in a while, I'll suddenly remember how gloriously saved I am. I always know it, of course. But sometimes, it comes to me like a news flash of late-breaking news. I'm reminded suddenly of what Jesus did for me on the cross, and I think, *I'm powerfully saved! I'm living forever in heaven with Jesus!* As I think about that, a chill rolls down my spine, and I feel elated and happy.

I think most of us are often guilty of taking our salvation for granted. We've become complacent about it, even though there is nothing on earth that could be better. I don't care if you win a billion dollars in the lottery, if you're named to *People* magazine's list of the sexiest people alive, or if you're a first-round draft pick of the Chicago Bears. There is nothing on earth that can remotely compare to the gift of eternal life!

Some people also make the mistake of believing that eternal life is something that starts later on, after we die, or after Jesus comes again. But I believe eternal life begins at the moment we accept Jesus as Savior. It starts right here on earth, in the life we're living right now. As Jesus said, "I have come that they might have life, and have it to the full" (John 10:10). Anyone who has the full life that Jesus offers should be a beacon of light pointing the way to Jesus through every means possible, including healings and other signs and wonders, as well as sharing the Gospel through words and deeds. As St. Francis of Assisi reportedly said, "Preach Jesus, and if necessary use words."

Good News! You're Rich!

In my book *Identity Thief*, I tell the story of a woman who had inherited many millions of dollars, but didn't know it. She was homeless for months, until the authorities finally found her to tell her that she was a rich woman. She was sleeping on sidewalks and fishing food out of dumpsters, when she could have been spending her nights sleeping on satin sheets in the finest hotels and eating in four-star restaurants.

Far too many believers are experiencing the spiritual equivalent of poverty and homelessness because they don't know that God has given them the ability and power to impact their neighborhoods, communities and cities for Christ.

As I mentioned earlier, it is often easy to tell when someone needs prayer for healing. He or she may be limping, coughing, feverish, emaciated or suffering in other visible ways. It's not as easy to spot those who need spiritual healing. They may look like they've got it all together. They might be right there in church with you on Sunday morning, joining in the worship and listening to the sermon, yet may never have made a personal profession of faith in Jesus. Or if they have, they haven't really made Him Lord.

In some ways, it can be even more difficult for us in our heads to talk to someone about Jesus than it is to ask that person if you can pray for him or her. The enemy will make us afraid of the rejection. But let me encourage you to go ahead and do it. After all, if someone is really saved, he or she will appreciate that you cared enough to share salvation. And, as I've said many times before, daring to share Jesus with anyone is well worth the risk.

Is Hell Real?

Does anybody believe hell is real? Several years ago, I attended a gathering of young leaders from Vineyard churches. The national overseer brought in a group of pastors who were under forty years of age to discuss various theological issues with three major theologians, one of whom attended a Vineyard church. One of the topics discussed at this gathering was, "Is there a literal hell?"

This meeting went on for three days, and by the end of this time, many of us were frustrated and exhausted by what seemed to us to be a constant attack against some very basic and fundamental Christian teachings.

I spoke up at one point and said, "If we really believed in hell, how would we be able to sleep at night if we knew we hadn't taken any action that day to prevent people from ending up in such a place for fifteen minutes—much less for all eternity? If we believe hell is real, we would devote every opportunity to telling people about Jesus so they wouldn't go there. Billy Graham once said, 'The worst thing about hell is the absence of God there. We have no idea how truly terrifying and awful that truly is.'"

Let me admit that I hate talking about hell. My ministry focuses on God's abundant grace, love and mercy for all people. I love sharing the good news that God loves us—so much so that Jesus was willing to suffer and die on our behalf—and that He wants the best for us in every situation. Because of what I know of God, I'm convinced that there wouldn't be a place called hell unless it was absolutely necessary. But as much as those theologians would like to pretend hell doesn't exist, Jesus said it does (see, for example, Matthew 25:41–46).

Suppose you woke up in the morning and smelled the strong, pungent odor of smoke. Then you looked out your window and saw flames shooting out of an upstairs window at the neighbors' house. What would you do? You'd run across the street as fast as you could, pounding on the door and screaming that their house was on fire. You'd keep at it until you were sure the people who lived there were outside and safe. If no one responded to your cries, you might try to break the door down or get in through a window. To sum it up, you'd do everything you possibly could to save those people from the fire.

I'll tell you what you wouldn't do if you looked out the window and saw your neighbors' house on fire. You wouldn't say, "Oh, well," and go back to sleep.

How, then, can we possibly ignore the situation when we have friends, neighbors and family members who don't know Christ, and who are possibly headed for hell? We can't!

Reaching Your *Oikos*

Oikos is a Greek word that basically means "house and family." But "family" in this context has a much broader meaning than we would normally attach to it. Your *oikos* includes your spouse and children, yes. But it also includes the eight to fifteen people you see almost every day, the ones who are clearly in your sphere of influence. This will include your friends (close or casual) in your neighborhood, as well as people like your co-workers, your mail carrier, the clerk at the local grocery store, your barber or hairdresser, the waiter you often see at your favorite restaurant, the people you work out with when you go to the gym—and so on.

These are the people that you and I should be influencing for Christ as we go through our daily walk with Him, at the very least. Of course, we should be doing as much as we can to share Jesus with everyone—but I believe that we have a special obligation to minister to the people we interact with on a regular basis.

The best thing you can do to touch these people for Jesus is to pray for them and allow them to experience His power.

What do you pray for? You can ask God to show you, and He will. Expect His answer. It may come right away, or it might take some time—especially if you are not used to hearing the voice of God.

I remember the first few times when I tried to wait quietly before the Lord. I'd attempt to clear my mind and ask Him to speak to me. Then, after waiting for what seemed like an hour, I'd look at my watch and see that I'd been listening for no more than five or ten minutes. I also found that my mind would wander. I'd think about all the things I had on my to-do list that day, start musing about something I'd seen on the news, or wonder how my favorite football team was doing. I really had to rein in my thoughts and keep them on the Lord.

I struggled, but finally succeeded in obeying the command of the apostle Paul to "take captive every thought" (2 Corinthians 10:5).

I also recall the first time I realized that if I got quiet and cleared away distractions, I could hear from God. Teresa Scott from my father's church came to me with a word from the Lord. The message she gave me was right on target, and my response was, "How did you know this?" I was flabbergasted when Teresa told me the Lord had spoken to her during her prayer time. I didn't know God spoke to people in any way outside the Bible. But He does, and all we have to do is ask and listen.

You know, a conversation isn't really a conversation if one person is doing all the talking. It's a monologue. Prayer is a conversation. It involves talking and listening. The person who doesn't spend time listening to God, the One who created the entire universe, is really missing out.

But what if God doesn't give you something specific to pray about with someone else? It's not hard to find something to pray about if you keep your eyes open. For instance:

- ▶ "I see you're struggling with a cold. Would you mind if I prayed for you right now?"
- ▶ "How's everything with your family these days? Anything I could pray about for you?"
- ▶ "Boy, a lot of people I know seem to be going through a tough time these days. Everything okay with you? Is there anything I could pray for?"
- ▶ "You seem to be limping a little bit. Can I pray for you right now?"

If you can't find something that leads naturally into prayer, you can just try the direct approach. Something like, "You know, Jesus loves you so much that He wants you to know by feeling His presence. Can I pray that you feel the tangible presence of God right now? Would that be all right?"

You can release the manifest presence of God by just saying, "I release heat . . . electricity . . . a weightiness of God's presence [etc.] over you so you will know how much Jesus loves you right now."

I've been shocked when I see what happens to people when I use the authority Jesus gave me in this way. And I know you'll be shocked, too. You want people to see God's hand at work *now*.

When we say, "I'll be praying for you," and then let it go, people may forget all about it. Even if God does something great for them, they may not recognize His hand in it. Again, we want to show them God's hand at work in their lives *now*!

On the Shoulders of Giants

One of the ways God strengthens me is through reading books written by heroes of the Christian faith, or through listening to their messages. I can stand on the shoulders of spiritual giants, and discovering what God did through them gives me faith that He can and will do the same thing through me. I hear His voice speaking through them and imparting faith into my heart and soul.

I want to be careful here, because I don't believe that it's faith that works through us to do great things for God. Rather, it is Christ in us, and His power and authority that we activate to do great things. We are merely His vessels. I'm speaking of faith here, and by faith I mean the belief that something will transform. Christians who think they are able to do anything because of *their* faith are misplacing their confidence. What I mean by this is that I believe our faith should be placed in Christ, and not in our faith—although I believe our faith is very important to the process.

The Bible does talk a great deal about the importance of faith. As we discussed earlier, there was an instance when Jesus couldn't perform many great miracles because of a lack of faith (belief in something transforming) on the part of the people in His hometown. Jesus said that anyone who had faith as small as a mustard seed could move mountains—literally. On more than one occasion, He told someone that the person's faith had made him or her whole.

Now, if you are willing to go out into the street and attempt to do the things that Jesus did, then you certainly have more than a mustard seed's worth of faith. I believe that anyone who prays to God has faith. If not, why be praying?

But if you struggle with prayer, or if you just can't bring yourself to go out and pray for others—to tell them about Jesus and let them know that He died for them—then it may be a big help to you to let God speak to you through the lives and works of people who undoubtedly belong in God's Hall of Heroes.

It may surprise you to know that some of my favorites are not exactly contemporaries, although there are many great men and women of faith serving God today. I love reading works by and about people like Brother Andrew and Watchman Nee.

Watchman Nee, who died nearly fifty years ago, blessed us with books like *The Normal Christian Life* and *Sit, Walk, Stand*. He was a valiant witness for Christ in China and was imprisoned by the Communist government.

After coming to Christ as a teenager, Watchman Nee sailed with several companions to the island village of Mei-hwa to share the Gospel. The villagers there were devoted to their local god, To-Wang. Nee and his companions arrived to find that on January 11, which was only a few days away, the whole island would come together to celebrate a festival in To-Wang's honor. This god's followers said that it had not rained on the day of the festival for almost three hundred years. Upon hearing this, one of Nee's companions said, "I promise you, our God, who is the true God, will make it rain on January 11."

At first, Watchman Nee was afraid that he and his friends might be putting God to the test. But as he prayed, he felt that God would, indeed, make it rain on the day of the festival, and that He wanted them to spread the word. So that's what they did. But when January 11 came around, the day was bright and sunny. Nee and his companions prayed that God would demonstrate His power, and as they were eating breakfast together, they heard the sound of raindrops falling on the roof. A few minutes later, the gentle rain turned into a downpour.

But that wasn't the end of the story. The high priest announced that he had made a mistake in calculating the day of the festival for To-Wang. The "real" date of the celebration was January 14—three days later. He insisted it would not rain on January 14, and that everyone would see that To-Wang was the true god.

As it turned out, the fourteenth was a repeat of the eleventh. The day dawned bright and sunny, with no clouds in the sky. But then a huge storm rolled in and drenched the island. Within weeks, a thriving Christian church had been established in Mei-hwa.[1]

I don't know about you, but I can't read stories like this one without being charged up and made ready for battle. I can hear God speaking to me, telling me to move forward and activate the authority Jesus gave me, and that He will be with me in every step.

Brother Andrew, a Dutch missionary nicknamed "God's Smuggler," would smuggle Bibles into the former Soviet Union, China and other nations where the Word of God was outlawed. He regularly prayed while crossing the border with hundreds of Bibles, *Lord, You made blind eyes see—now make seeing eyes blind to these Bibles.* It worked! Again and again it would happen.

I was ministering recently with my friend Todd White when the pastor came up and told me, "Brother Andrew's grandchildren would like to meet you." I was thrilled. I had heard Brother Andrew speak when I was seven years old, and I still recall several of the stories he shared that night. After hearing him speak, I told my parents, "I want to be him when I grow up." Now these grandkids of my superhero wanted to meet me. What an honor!

When the children's father said to me, "They are fans of your ministry and ask for an impartation from you; they want to be like you," I nearly swallowed my own tongue! When I met the kids, their eyes were huge with wonder. I thought about Thor, my newly born grandson, who was one day old at the time, and I wondered, *Whom will Thor Dawkins want to meet and get an impartation from?*

Maybe it's you, the one reading these words right now.

YOUR ACTIVATION GUIDE

- ▶ What does it mean to you to be saved? How does this impact the way you live your life?
- ▶ How often do you share your faith with others? If you struggle in this area, start praying that God will lead you to people who need to know about salvation through faith in Christ.
- ▶ Make a list of some of the people you meet frequently who need to hear God's offer of eternal life through His Son.
- ▶ List some of the ways you can bring a conversation around to a person's need for Jesus.
- ▶ Do you have some friends who share your desire to transform lives for God's Kingdom? If so, get together with them and practice putting Jesus on display. Although I believe in being led by the Holy Spirit, I also know we aren't waiting on the Holy Spirit to act.

Stories from the Battlefield

I heard you speak, but was skeptical. Then I saw blind eyes open and felt something shift like the foundational beams of my spirit. . . . After that, I went on a healing frenzy—saw arches raise, headaches clear, backs straighten, etc.

Then, by God's grace, I got on a flight to Chicago and found myself sitting next to you! I got to ask you lots of questions, and you answered them all. Since then I've seen legs grow out, blind eyes open, and deaf ears open. I've seen demons flee, had children pray (as I saw you do) for a broken wrist that was made new before our eyes, and have seen countless people's pain leave.

One girl who was tormented by schizophrenia was delivered and taken off her meds by her doctors, and I just witnessed my first creative miracle, with a woman's finger growing a full centimeter as a friend and I prayed for her. This is who I am now: a normal Christian. Jesus used you to change my life.

—Emily Ables

7

Vanquish Demons

Put on the full armor of God, so that you can take your stand against the devil's schemes. For our struggle is not against flesh and blood, but against the rulers, against the authorities, against the powers of this dark world and against the spiritual forces of evil in the heavenly realms.

Ephesians 6:11–12

I've been dealing with demons all my life. Satan knew, before I was born, that God was going to use me to preach the Gospel, and he was determined not to let that happen. He appeared to my mother every month while she was pregnant with me, threatening to kill both her and me if she dared to carry the pregnancy to full term. He made the same threat to my father, although my dad only saw him face-to-face on one occasion.

I believe it was only the power and protection of God that kept him from carrying out those threats. My mom and I both survived, as an angel told her we would. But the devil wasn't done with me. When I was an adolescent, I endured a long period of being tormented by demonic activity in my room at night. I understood that the devil was no match for God's power. But still, when it was dark in my room and the dread, fear and evil were so real that I could reach out and touch them, I had demons choke me, poke me and even drag me off my bed. It could be hard to remember that He who was in me was greater than he who is in the world (see 1 John 4:4).

And, no, it was not my imagination. One of the most frightening experiences of my life occurred when I woke up in the middle of the night, opened my eyes and became aware that the ceiling was only a few inches away from my face. An evil presence in my room had caused me to levitate above my bed.

I wrote about being levitated by demonic power in my book *Identity Thief*, so I won't go back over it in detail now. Suffice it to say that I discovered that Satan and his demons are real, but they are no match for the power that is ours through Christ.

The truth is that all human beings were born into a war, and we're either on God's side or the devil's side. There are no conscientious objectors in this war. No neutral territories. We might prefer to stay on the sidelines, far away from the battlefield, but we can't. If you try to stay out of the battle, Satan's troops will bring it to you.

As I look out my window today, it's a bright, sunny day here in Illinois. It's the middle of winter, but we've been blessed with some unseasonably warm weather. The sky is blue, with a few puffy, white clouds. It's a day when the whole world seems at peace. But it's not. Even though I can't see it, I know that underneath the peaceful scene outside my window, a ferocious battle between good and evil is raging.

Now, it may be bad news to you that you're a soldier in a war, whether you like it or not. But I do have some good news as well. If you belong to Jesus, you are fighting on the winning side and the enemy can't hurt you. In fact, he has already been defeated by Christ's death, burial and resurrection. He refuses to lay down his arms, but his ultimate annihilation is inevitable.

Demons can put on a scary show. They can moan and wail and rattle chains in the middle of the night to scare us. I've seen demons make their victims get down on the ground and crawl like animals and slither around like snakes. I've heard them speak through people in voices so scary that they make a heavy metal singer sound like Mickey Mouse in comparison. I've seen them do all sorts of eerie and scary things.

But I've never seen a demon stand up to the power and authority of Jesus Christ. And when I read through the Bible, I never find a time where Jesus was afraid of a demon. It was always the other way around. Demons begged Him to leave them alone. They asked Him to go away from them. Whenever Jesus came around, they were terrified. If you are His ambassador, filled with His Spirit, they are terrified of you, too.

It would take another entire book to discuss deliverance ministry in detail, but there are a few other important things I want to tell you. Here are some basics to get you started:

1. *Demons are cunning.* They will try everything they can to confuse and fool you. For this reason, when starting out in this area of going into an open confrontation with a demon or demons, if possible, it is best to have someone with you who has had some experience in deliverance ministry.

2. *Demons do not know everything about you.* They can try to bring up sin that you have not repented for and try to make you think that you are not worthy of the name "Christian." Don't listen. You are worthy because of Christ's work. He died to cover your sins. If anything is still not covered, then pray and sincerely cover it.

3. *If demons are manifesting, command them in Jesus' name to stop.* If they are speaking in scary voices or causing

people to crawl around on the floor, make wild eyes at you, and levitate, or if they are generally causing havoc in other ways (which are some of the devil's intimidation tactics), command them in the name of Jesus to stop manifesting. This will make it much easier to deal with them. The demonic manifestation is only an abuse of the host person and an intimidation tactic.

4. *Finally, command the demon or demons to be bound, to leave in the name of Jesus and to go wherever the Lord Jesus Christ, who came in the flesh, commands them to go.* If a Spirit-filled believer commands them in Jesus' name to go, they have no choice but to obey.

Stay Alert at All Times

You never know where the devil is going to show up.

Or what disguise he's going to be wearing.

The apostle Paul said Satan sometimes tries to disguise himself as an angel of light. Other times, he boldly announces his true identity, or hides and hopes that no one will notice him. As C. S. Lewis said, there are two big mistakes that most people make when it comes the devil. The first mistake is thinking about him too much. The second mistake is not thinking about him enough.[1]

In other words, it's dangerous to give him too much credit. But it can be just as bad to give him too little credit. He and his demons are real. They are responsible for much of the trouble, sorrow and pain in the world today.

The good news is that there is no demon anywhere, including Satan himself, who can withstand the power of Jesus Christ.

The same Jesus who told us to heal the sick and raise the dead also told us to cast out demons, and 1 John 3:8 tells us that the Son of God came into this world to destroy the works of the devil. Jesus also said that the gates of hell would not be able to withstand the power of His Church.

But you can't fight demons if you don't know they exist.

Too Sophisticated to Believe in Demons?

Many people in our "sophisticated" age don't believe in demons. They believe, instead, only in psychological disorders such as paranoid schizophrenia and such. But Jesus certainly believed in demons and often battled them during His earthly ministry. I believe that demons exist, because Jesus said they do. And I believe in demons because I, too, have come face-to-face with them, battled them and defeated them in the powerful name of Jesus.

I also believe in the existence of mental disorders and psychological problems. Sometimes it can be difficult to tell the difference between illness and demonic possession or harassment. It can take lots of prayer, especially for discernment. Remember that we have God's promise that if we ask Him for wisdom, He will give it to us (see James 1:5). Why do you need to know whether or not demons are involved? Because it won't do any good to cast demons out of a person when there are no demons. Nor will it totally help to pray for healing when the true problem is demonic in origin.

Yet even though this is true, I also believe that there can be a strong link between psychological disorders and demonic persecution. I have asked psychologists about it, and they've told me that there is often a strong "anti-God" flavor to schizophrenia.

I've been blessed to see two people completely healed of schizophrenia. In both instances, their psychiatrists took them off their medications and declared them totally cured through prayer. One of these healings occurred during a worship service. The other took place in a grocery store I was visiting. You never know where the battle will arise!

The voices these people hear may express a violent hatred toward God. The voices may also urge their victims to curse God, tell them that they don't need God, or tell them that God doesn't exist.

It seems to me that you'd have to be foolish to believe that this kind of blasphemous behavior is merely coincidental. Besides, I defy anyone to read through a newspaper or watch the evening news and come away doubting the existence of demons. Demons are real . . . but you have power over them.

The Devil in L.A.

Late last year, when I spoke at a church in Los Angeles, a young woman came seeking healing for severe neck and shoulder pain. She was of Asian descent and spoke only her home tongue, so a friend who had accompanied her to the service that evening translated everything she told me. With the friend's help, I also learned that the lady was dealing with severe sinus pressure that made her eyes burn and caused her vision to blur.

On this particular night one of my many friends, a man who pastors a church in the San Diego area, had driven more than 100 miles north to attend the service in Los Angeles. His children were with him, and I was delighted to see them, as always. I know that children are special to Jesus, who even said that no one could enter God's Kingdom unless he or she became like a little child (see Matthew 18:3). That's why I love to invite children to come up onstage and help me minister healing to people who are sick and suffering. On this occasion I asked one of my friend's boys, who was about ten years old, to join me.

As I usually do, I asked the boy to put his hands on the woman's back and repeat after me as I prayed for her healing. Almost immediately, her pain level dropped from a 10 to a

3. We prayed again . . . but this time our prayer did not have the desired effect. Far from it.

The lady suddenly gasped and grabbed her shoulder. The pain was back in full force. In fact, it was worse than ever—up to a 15!

I immediately knew that the devil had his claws in her and was fighting with everything he had to hang on to her. I know that when I pray for someone and the pain gets worse, it's a sure sign of demonic involvement. It's like you're pulling something away from the demon, and he digs in even harder.

The woman was grabbing her head and neck, and she seemed to be in agony. We prayed again, but the pain only got worse.

My friend's young son looked at me as if to ask, "What do I do now?"

"Don't worry," I told him. "Repeat after me: In the name of Jesus, I bind you, spirit of infirmity and death!"

As soon as those words came out of the child's mouth, the woman crumpled to the floor. She also began wailing and screaming in a loud voice. Her eyes were shut tightly, and she covered them with her hands as she writhed on the floor. When I asked her friend to find out what was going on, the woman replied that the pain in her neck and shoulders had subsided somewhat—but the pressure behind her eyes had escalated to the point where she thought they were about to pop out of her head.

My young partner and I commanded the demon to stop manifesting, and then we told it to depart in the name of Jesus. I'll have to admit, in fact, that the young man was being a lot more forceful with his prayers than I was.

"In the *name* of Jesus . . . I *command* you to come *out!*"

He was emphasizing his words and enunciating like a TV evangelist, which is not exactly his father's style at all. It was amazing to see a ten-year-old boy pray with such fervency. And as he commanded, the lady stopped screaming and lay still on the floor.

"How are you now?" I asked.

She sat up, opened her eyes and said something in her native language.

"She says it's all gone," her friend interpreted. "The pain, the pressure—it's all gone."

I held out my hand and helped her to her feet.

"There's one more thing we have to do," I told her. We prayed together, in the name of Jesus, and forbade the demon from ever returning.

That final step is so important, but unfortunately, it's one many people overlook. If you don't specifically forbid a demon from returning to its victim, and tell it to go to the feet of Jesus for judgment, there is no guarantee that it will stay away. As Jesus says in Matthew 12:43–45,

> When an impure spirit comes out of a person, it goes through arid places seeking rest and does not find it. Then it says, "I will return to the house I left." When it arrives, it finds the house unoccupied, swept clean and put in order. Then it goes and takes with it seven other spirits more wicked than itself, and they go in and live there. And the final condition of that person is worse than the first.

In talking to the woman's friends and family after the service that night, I discovered that she had been suffering from intense back and shoulder pain for years. There had been no accident or injury. Rather, it had apparently come as the result of a spiritual attack unleashed by an antagonistic family member who still lived in the woman's native country. This person was also considered to be a conjurer of spirits, and he had put a curse on his relative because of some perceived slight.

As I'm writing this, it has been only about six weeks since that deliverance. It's been about two weeks since I have received an email from the woman's family, but at that point they reported that she was doing fine, and I have no reason to think that she won't continue to be free from pain—praise God!

Jumping Out of a Wheelchair

I was speaking at a church called Beach Chapel in San Diego. Historically, Beach Chapel had been part of the cessationist movement, which, as you may remember, is the teaching that miracles came for the purpose of establishing the Church in the first century, but that they no longer exist today.

In recent years, the church's opposition to healing and miracles has softened quite a bit—which pretty much explains why I was invited to come there on a weekend to teach a group how to go out into their community and do the things that Jesus did.

On the first night of a conference like this, I'll usually call for people who have back or shoulder injuries or other "lesser" problems to come forward for healing. People occasionally ask me, "Why don't you call up people who have cancer or heart disease, or who are blind or in wheelchairs?"

My answer is that it's because—in addition to bringing healing to people and showing the power of Jesus—I am also striving to give people the faith and boldness they need to reach out and provide healing in the name of Jesus. If I went right after someone who was paralyzed and had been in a wheelchair for years, the average person might think, *I could never do that*, and lose heart. But when people see someone healed from back pain or something similar, they are more likely to think, *I can do that!* In other words, I purposely try to pull back in order to give people the faith to do what I do.

The first night at Beach Chapel, one particular man in a wheelchair was pushed into the meeting and parked in the first row. He was curled up in that chair, and I got the impression that he couldn't even move. As a matter of fact, I noticed that his head kept drooping over to one side. Whenever that happened, the person attending him would gently lift it back up. But it wouldn't stay that way very long.

I discovered later that this gentleman had contracted a particular disease that had caused him to lose all muscular function. I was told that due to the disease, he had become totally incapacitated.

Everything within me wanted to pray for this poor fellow. But I held back because I felt as though I needed to "start small" for the reasons I just gave you. Instead of starting with the fellow in the wheelchair, I asked for people to come forward if they needed healing for back pain, and a dozen responded.

My experience has been that in a situation like this, healing usually comes fairly quickly. But that night, this was not the case. People's pain levels were going down as they were prayed for, but almost imperceptibly. Instead of going down from a 10 to 0, or from a 10 to a 1 or 2, they were dropping from 10 to 9½, and then from 9½ to 8½, and so on.

We finally reached the point where most of the people had gone down to a pain level of 1 or a little bit above that, but nobody had been completely healed. And there were three people whose levels had gone down to around 6 but wouldn't drop any lower.

I felt frustrated and exhausted, as if I was involved in some terrible struggle and didn't have a whole lot to show for it. And there, on the front row, sat the poor fellow in the wheelchair. Satan seemed to be mocking me: *You can't even heal a few people with back pain. What makes you think you could do anything for someone whose body has been ravaged by this disease?*

Then I realized that being involved in a terrible struggle was exactly what was going on. I was in a war with demons! And they were not about to give up easily. I was angry as I left the building that night and vowed that, with God's grace, tomorrow would be different.

The next morning, Angie and I were having a buffet breakfast at our hotel, along with our son Judah and his wife, Evangelina, when I noticed that the woman who was keeping the buffet stocked up seemed to have a bad back. She was working so hard, but it hurt me to see the way she moved.

I told Angie I was going to go pray for the woman, but she had a better idea. "That's great, but don't do it right now."

"Why not?"

"She's so busy, and I don't want her to get in trouble because her boss thinks she's slacking off or anything like that. Why don't you wait until it slows down in here?"

Angie was right. But I was determined that I was going to pray for the woman at the first opportunity. I waited in the lobby, occasionally spying on her to see how the breakfast was going. (It's a good thing she didn't notice that I was "stalking" her. It wouldn't have done much for my reputation to have a run-in with a couple of hotel security guards.) I admit that I had three goals in mind:

1. to set a woman free from the pain Satan had inflicted upon her for years
2. to show the power and mercy of Jesus Christ
3. to exact a toll on the demons who were fighting so hard to keep people in bondage—to make them pay for their opposition of the previous night

Finally, the time scheduled for breakfast came to an end and the dining room cleared out. My time had come. I went in and told her that I had been watching the way she walked, and it appeared that she was dealing with severe pain in her lower back or hip.

She gave me a blank look, as if she didn't know what I was talking about. And it turned out that she didn't. She didn't speak English—only Spanish. I've spent enough time traveling in Latin America to be able to speak a bit of what I call "survival Spanish." Through that, I was able to determine that yes, she was in quite a bit of pain.

Gesturing to her that I would be right back, I went and found a maintenance worker who spoke both English and Spanish, and I asked him if he would translate for me. With his help, I said to her, "I think you have one leg that's shorter than the other."

She looked puzzled. "I don't know," she replied.

I asked her if she would mind sitting down and extending her legs so we could check. When she did, it was clear that one of her legs was nearly three-quarters of an inch shorter than the other one.

Just as I was asking her if she would let me pray for her, Judah happened to walk into the room.

"Hey, Dad," he said, holding up his cell phone, "why don't we do this live on Facebook?"

I thought it was a good idea, and the woman agreed that she would be happy to do it. Now, I hope you understand that in a situation like this, my desire is never to draw attention to myself or to boost my ministry. My intention is always to bring glory to Jesus and, by showing what He can do, let the world know that He is indeed the King of kings and Lord of lords. I encourage others to do the same.

We began praying for her, and at first—just like the night before—nothing happened.

I gritted my teeth. I was determined that the angels of darkness were not going to defeat us. No matter how long it took, I would keep on praying until victory was achieved. It didn't take long. When healing came, it came suddenly. Her short leg suddenly experienced a dramatic growth spurt and became the same length as the other leg.

I asked her to walk around and try it out, which she did with ease, before reporting to me that the pain was completely gone.

While Judah and I had been praying for this woman, one of her co-workers had come out of the kitchen to watch. I sensed that she had a problem with one of her hips, and I asked her about it.

"Oh yes," she said. "I have a mass on my hip." She didn't know what it was, but feared that it might be cancer. "Here," she gestured for me to put my hand on her hip. "Feel it."

When I was hesitant to do that, she came up with another idea. She put her hands on her hips and asked me to put my own hands on top of them and press. When I did, I could feel a significant difference. There was definitely some sort of large growth on her left hip.

As soon as we started praying, she exclaimed, "It's getting smaller! I can feel it shrinking!"

She began walking around the room, and as she did, the mass continued to shrink. After a few minutes, she stopped and began rubbing her hip. "It's gone!" she said.

"Are you sure?"

"Yes! Come see for yourself!"

Once again, she put her hands on her hips and asked me to push on them. Both sides felt the same. She had been healed in a matter of moments. Grateful tears rolled down her cheeks, and I felt certain this was a turning point in the "Battle of Beach Chapel."

Rise Up, O Man of God

That evening, the second night of the conference, we opened with a time of worship and praise led by Judah and Evangelina, and then I got up to speak. Once again, the man in the wheelchair was sitting on the front row. I decided immediately that the things I had prepared to say could wait. This was a time for action.

"You know what?" I asked. "Before we do anything else, how many of you want to see this man healed?"

The reaction was mixed. Everybody wanted to see it happen. But most of the people were hesitant, because they didn't seem to think it *would* happen. If I prayed for the guy and nothing changed, it would be an embarrassment and put a damper on the entire evening. How could I teach them how to heal in the name of Jesus if I couldn't do it myself?

"Come on," I said. "Let's pray for him."

I walked over to the wheelchair and asked, "Could we pray for you?"

I wasn't surprised that he didn't respond, because I really didn't think he could move. Even so, I reached down, put my hand on his chest and said, "You foul spirit of sickness and death, I bind you now in the name of Jesus. I command this body to be restored." Then I shouted out a phrase from a song we used to sing when I was kid: "Rise up, O man of God!"

As soon as I said that, he started rocking back and forth.

"Rise up now!" I shouted.

Immediately, he leapt out of the wheelchair and started to run!

I hate to admit it, but it scared me. I had expected him to stand up and walk, but I never thought he was going to shoot out of that wheelchair like an Olympic sprinter when the starting pistol is fired.

Instinctively, I grabbed his shirt to keep him from doing a face-plant on the floor of the auditorium.

"Let him go! Let him go!" His caregiver was jumping up and down in excitement. "I've never seen him like this!"

I let go and he took off. If I hadn't let go, I'm pretty sure he would have run right out of that shirt. He began running laps around the auditorium at a pretty fast clip. His legs were so emaciated that I didn't see how in the world they could hold his body up—much less carry him around the sanctuary at top speed—but they did. After several trips around the place, he plopped down on the front row, panting and huffing like a locomotive. I was certain that he'd used up every ounce of strength.

I went over to see if he was okay. And . . . to my astonishment, he sprang out of that chair and starting sprinting around the auditorium again! I couldn't help but think of the verse from Isaiah: "Those who hope in the LORD will renew their strength. They will soar on wings like eagles; they will run and not grow weary, they will walk and not be faint" (Isaiah 40:31). I also remembered the movie *Forrest Gump*, where the title character spent weeks running back and forth across the United States. I wondered if this man was ever going to stop!

It may be strange for me to talk about the prophet Isaiah and Forrest Gump in the same paragraph. They don't really have anything to do with each other. But just the same, I had to keep myself from yelling, "Run, Forrest, run!"

I was so stunned by what I was seeing that I couldn't even remember the things I had prepared to talk about that night. I've seen more dramatic healings, but never one that caused such a stir!

Finally, the running came to an end. The "crippled" man again sat down on the front row, a huge grin spread across his face. His body was erect. He held his head high.

The enemy had been defeated and the floodgates of healing had opened. We had also shown Satan and his demons that we would never give up or back down. There were dozens of other healings that night. Legs and arms grew out. Backs, necks and shoulders were healed. Many people were rescued from Satan's grip and had their faith activated to do for others what God had done for them.

Unfortunately, I didn't get to talk to the "wheelchair guy" that night, because, as you can imagine, at the end of a service like that I am surrounded by people who need prayer or who just want to talk to me about something I said. However, Judah and Evangelina were able to talk to the man and his caregiver before they left, and reported that they were both overjoyed by what had happened. In fact, the caregiver told Evangelina that before that night, her client had not been able to use his vocal cords in several weeks. Tonight, although his speech was a little shaky, he was able to express his gratitude to God in his own voice, as his eyes overflowed with tears. Praise God, he left the church pushing his own wheelchair.

From San Diego, my family and I headed north to Laguna Niguel, where I spoke at a Vineyard church on Sunday morning and Monday night. At the second service, somebody who looked very familiar to me came through the back door just as the service was starting. I knew him, but I couldn't quite place him. It wasn't until near the end of the service that I recognized that he was the fellow who had jumped out of the wheelchair at Beach Chapel. I didn't recognize him without his wheelchair! I wanted to talk to him, but he again left before I had an opportunity to do so.

The Finger of God

Sometimes demons stay behind the scenes. When Angie and I launched a church in Aurora, Illinois, we prayed that God would not allow any demons to come through the doors into our sanctuary.

That was a mistake.

There were plenty of demons in Aurora—just as there are plenty of demons in every city throughout the United States and the world. But the problem was especially severe in Aurora, a city plagued with crime, drug addiction, prostitution, gang violence and poverty. It was listed as one of the top ten most dangerous cities in the United States at the time that we planted the church there. Hundreds of people in Aurora needed to be set free from demonic oppression and posses-sion. By closing the doors of our church to them, we had pre-vented them from coming to God's house, where they could obtain the deliverance they needed so desperately.

One young man I'll call Hector eventually was set free after a long and difficult struggle with demonic bondage. He told us that he had tried six times to come to our church, but he could never get through the door. "Something" always com-pelled him to turn around and leave.

When we realized what we had done, we prayed, "Lord, if people with demons are coming to us because they want to be set free, then let them come." After that, a steady stream of men and women who were being tormented by demons came through those doors, and they walked out again as new creatures in Christ.

Hector was a member of one of the city's powerful gangs. He had actually come to Aurora because he was wanted by the police in his hometown in another state. He was one of those guys who, if you looked at his life story, might cause you to say, "Poor guy never had a chance."

Hector was born in prison to a woman who was addicted to heroin. At the age of five, he was suspended from kin-dergarten for bringing a knife to school. At eight, he was expelled for coming to school with a gun. From the time he had been old enough to choose between right and wrong, he had been involved in violence, drugs and open rebellion against God. He lived the sort of life that is kind of like hang-ing out a welcome mat that says, "Demons welcome."

Like I said, when Angie and I first met him, Hector was in his early twenties. His girlfriend, Rosa, was even younger and was pregnant with their third child. They lived in a shabby apartment in a rundown high-rise in Aurora. Hector wanted to try to live for God, but he struggled for a number of rea-sons, one of them being that he didn't know how to make an honest living. Gangbanging was all he had ever known. And although he was trying to overcome his past, he still felt the pull of meth and other illegal drugs.

This all came to a head one afternoon when Angie took our sons to visit Rosa. Angie knew that Rosa and her kids didn't get out very much, and she wanted to show them a fun afternoon. Angie had to ring the bell a long time before Rosa came to the door. When she finally did, Angie was shocked to see that her face was bruised and her clothes were torn. She didn't have to ask what had happened. Hector had beaten Rosa up because she wouldn't tell him where the money was that a family member had sent Rosa to buy formula for their youngest.

Angie was furious. And believe me, you don't want to make Angie furious.

She said, "You're coming home with me. Boys, help her get her things together."

Of course, there were already eight of us in our house— Angie, our six boys and me. Now there would be eleven, and one on the way—quite a houseful. But Angie didn't care about that. Rosa and her children needed a safe place to stay, and Angie was determined to give them one. And as far as I was concerned, well, she thought she'd tell me about it later—perhaps at the dinner table on Saturday evening when I got back from Los Angeles, where I was meeting with some mission leaders.

Rosa was happy that she had a place to go, but she was also very scared.

"I'm afraid Hector will hurt you if he finds out you've helped me," she protested. "He's dangerous. You know, he carries a gun."

"I'm not worried about that," Angie said. "He doesn't understand how powerful my God is."

"But he may be out there. Please don't let him see you. I mean it!"

The two women made it down the old, slow elevator, which wasn't an easy thing to do, considering that they were carrying a baby and had seven other children with them. Not to mention that as you might suspect in a neighborhood like this one, the elevator didn't even work properly. It was practically out of order.

They finally made it out to the street and headed for Angie's van. But before they got there, they saw Hector on the other side of the street. He had his back turned to them and was talking on his cell phone while leaning against a telephone pole.

"Don't," Rosa whispered, reaching out in an attempt to grab Angie's arm and stop her from confronting her "armed and dangerous" boyfriend.

But it was too late.

Have I mentioned that it's not a good idea to make Angie mad?

Angie stormed across the street, grabbed Hector by the shoulder and spun him around to face her. As he did, she slapped the cell phone out of his hand and into the street, while holding his baby in her arms the entire time.

She wagged her finger in his face and shouted, "You listen to me! You've been beating that girl, and that's gonna stop. I'm taking her home with me, and if you know what's good for you, you'll stay away. Do you understand me? I'll deal with you later!"

Having said her piece, she stomped off toward Rosa and the children. Hector just stood there as if he were frozen to the spot, watching her go.

I flew back in from Los Angeles on Saturday. Sunday morning as I arrived at church, our worship pastor was waiting for me.

"Hey, Robby!" he said, "Hector is up there in your office right now. And he seems jacked up."

"Oh man!" I didn't want to deal with this right then, especially just before the Sunday morning service was about to start.

"Do you want me to come up there with you?" he asked.

"Nah, I'll take care of it."

I trudged up the stairs to my office, looked in and saw Hector sitting there, shaking as if he had the dt's. But he wasn't detoxing; he was scared.

As soon as he saw me, he jumped up and came toward me, his eyes huge with fear. "Is Angie here?"

"Yeah," I said. "She's downstairs."

He reached over and shut the door behind me.

"Dude, I've been shot, I've been stabbed, but I've never been so scared as I was when she put that finger in my face and began to wag it."

I dropped my shoulders and looked compassionately at him. "Yes, I'm quite familiar with that finger."

"I mean it," he said. "I can't eat. I can't sleep. I can't do anything. What's wrong with me? Every time I close my eyes, I see her face and that finger."

"She put the fear of God on you."

He cocked his head and said, "Well, I've heard people say that, but I never knew—"

"They're just talking," I interrupted. "She actually has put the real terror of God on you! And the only way to remove it is to have her pray for you."

He wasn't too sure about that. "Does she have to be in the room to do that?" he asked.

"Yes," I said. It was the only thing that could be done for him, so he agreed that I could invite her to join our conversation.

Hector always wore a baseball cap and shades, and when Angie came through the door, he stood to his feet, grabbed it off his head and put it over his heart, as if he were pledging allegiance to the flag.

When I saw that, I had to struggle not to laugh. But Angie was in no laughing mood. When I explained that I wanted her to pray for Hector, all the old anger rose up inside her. She began wagging her finger at him as he blurted out, "Oh no!"

"Why should I release you?" she asked. "You beat up innocent little girls!"

He tightened his grip on his cap and backed away. "I swear, it will never happen again. I swear it!"

Angie put her hands on her hips and glared at him. "You'd better say never!"

"It won't! I swear!"

"Sit down!" Angie was starting to soften, but she was still angry enough to be scary.

Hector sat down abruptly, and Angie moved toward him. When she reached her arms out in his direction, he flinched—just a little. But when he realized she was just going to put her hands on his shoulders so she could pray for him, he relaxed. As she prayed for him, God's presence came into the room, and we were all enveloped in peace. All fear and anger faded away in God's soothing, healing presence.

Hector had made a promise that he would never hurt Rosa again, and he kept it. He had never known how to be tender with a woman or to show her that he loved her and cared for her. He had to learn, and that's what he did. Rosa lived with us for the next several months while Hector learned how to court her. Angie told him he wasn't allowed to see Rosa or the kids if he didn't show up to our house with flowers in his hand for her and a massive apology.

He did, and when he came to our place for dinner on Monday night, we worked with him on how to act like a gentleman. He took Rosa on dates and told her how much he cared for her. Before they had any children, the only time he had come to see her—while she was living in a tent in someone's backyard—was when he wanted to have sex with her. Sometimes, as we worked with him, I felt, *This must be what it's like to work with people who've been raised by wolves.* But we kept at it because we knew Jesus wanted to transform Hector into His own likeness.

Near the end of her pregnancy, Hector asked Rosa to marry him, and she accepted. Angie took this very pregnant girl to a prom dress outlet store to find something that looked like a wedding dress. They were thumbing through light blues and pinks when Rosa turned to Angie and said, "I know I don't deserve it at all. But do you think it would be okay if I bought a white dress for my wedding?"

Angie's eyes welled up with tears. It had been a long uphill journey, but she put her hand on Rosa's shoulder and said, "I think Jesus wants you to wear white at your wedding."

It was my privilege and honor to perform their wedding ceremony . . . and baptize them on the same day.

There had been many bumps and hold-your-breath moments along the way. But after a couple of years they moved back to Hector's home state, and last we heard from them, they were happily married and following Jesus with all their might.

Now, you may be thinking, *There were no demons in Hector's story.*

Oh yes, there were. Hector was surrounded by them. Spirits of drug addiction, violence and promiscuity were all around him. Some in his family were well-known witches in the Chicago area. My purpose in telling you his story is to remind you that there is no power on earth stronger than the love and mercy of God. It's actually fun to go into the world's darkest places and see God show up and go to work. Never forget what Jesus said: "I am the light of the world. Whoever follows me will never walk in darkness, but will have the light of life" (John 8:12).

YOUR ACTIVATION GUIDE

► Have you asked God to fill you with His Holy Spirit? This is vital for any Christian, and especially for those who are engaged in a face-to-face battle with demons. Luke 11:13 says, "If you then, though you are evil, know how to give good gifts to your children, how much more will your Father in heaven give the Holy Spirit to those who ask him!"

▸ The apostle John writes that the One who is in you is greater than the one who is in the world. What does this mean to you?

▸ Prayerfully seek God about whether or not He is calling you to get involved in deliverance ministry. Whereas I believe all Christians should be prepared to take part in deliverance when necessary, some may be called to concentrate on this particular area.

▸ Does your church have a deliverance ministry? If so, perhaps you can consider getting involved and learning from those with experience in this area. If there is no deliverance ministry, consider talking to your pastor or other spiritual leader about starting one.

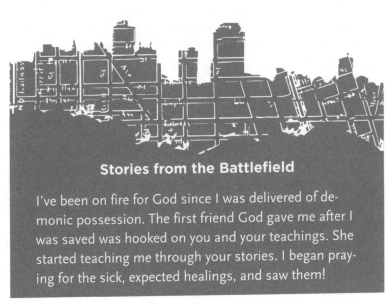

Stories from the Battlefield

I've been on fire for God since I was delivered of demonic possession. The first friend God gave me after I was saved was hooked on you and your teachings. She started teaching me through your stories. I began praying for the sick, expected healings, and saw them!

One of my favorites came while I was on the God Mobile at the state fair. A lady came up for prayer and I noticed she had terrible holes in her arms and blisters filled with pus. Although she was asking for prayer for her son, I asked if I could pray for her arms and she said yes. I put my hands out to touch her, but she recoiled and told me not to touch her because she was afraid I would get whatever she had. Still, I held her arms and prayed to a God who listens.

The next day, she came back to show me what had happened. There was not one scar, blister, or boil. She was healed. Her arms were beautiful, nearly glowing. I see her every year at the fair, and I call her the peach lady because she brings me peaches.

—Phebe Bell

PART THREE

MORE
WEAPONS
FOR YOUR
ARSENAL

8

Practicing Discernment

And this is my prayer: that your love may abound more
and more in knowledge and depth of insight, so that
you may be able to discern what is best and may be pure
and blameless for the day of Christ, filled with the fruit
of righteousness that comes through Jesus Christ—to
the glory and praise of God.

Philippians 1:9–11

Frank had a horrible cough.

He was one of those guys who coughed so much that
it annoyed everybody around him. One of those dry, hacking
things that made him sound pretty much like those sea lions
that like to congregate on the wharf at San Francisco.

People were always coming up and giving Frank advice
regarding which medicine could silence that bark of his once
and for all. Cold-EEZE, Ricola, Robitussin—you name it, he
tried them all, and nothing worked.

He also told me he tried prayer, but that didn't work either.
He was increasingly discouraged, because he knew that God

had the power to raise the dead and heal diseases like leprosy and cancer, but He couldn't or wouldn't seem to do a thing about that cough.

Frank, who was probably in his midsixties when I met him and he asked me for prayer, didn't have a lot of faith left that he would ever be healed. Perhaps coughing was his "thorn in the flesh" and he'd never be free, he said. But I knew better. The God I serve wouldn't ruin someone's life with a hacking cough. He just wouldn't!

As soon as I laid hands on Frank and began to pray for him, I sensed a dark presence.

I asked Frank if there was anything in his background that might have opened him up to demonic activity. He couldn't think of anything. But our conversation gradually came around to me asking if this was a generational issue.

He said, "Well, my father had it, and his father and my great-grandfather. They all had this cough. We jokingly call it the Miller Men's Curse. As a matter of fact, we'd all cough so bad that we would pass out."

Frank's cough wasn't caused by an illness. It was the result of a real curse and demonic oppression. In other words, he didn't need to be healed, but delivered.

In the name of Jesus, I commanded that "the Miller Curse be broken and the demons causing Frank to cough leave him now!"

What happened next is going to sound crazy, but it's absolutely true. Frank coughed really hard, and what looked like a full-grown gorilla jumped out of his chest and ran through the wall and out of the building. There were about ten of us there who saw it.

After this, he dropped to his knees and shouted, "It's gone!"

Frank has never struggled with it again, and that was five years ago. In that instance when we prayed, God was giving me discernment to ask about Frank's family history.

Getting Discernment

In part two of this book, we discussed the fact that we are all soldiers in the war between good and evil. Even the person who insists that he or she is not going to take sides has, by not choosing, chosen a side. In other words, if you're not on God's side, you're on the enemy's side by default.

Over the past several chapters, we've talked specifically how we can go out on the streets and do the things that Jesus did during His three years of earthly ministry:

► heal the sick
► prophesy
► raise the dead
► cast out demons
► bring people into God's Kingdom

In the pages ahead, I want to share some of the other things I've learned as I've traveled the world, following in Christ's footsteps, namely:

► how to acquire discernment
► what to do when the devil fights back
► why God sometimes seems to say no
► gaining victory in Jesus
► why God loves atheists

Let's start with discernment, and I'll cut right to the chase. A lack of discernment is one of the biggest problems in the Church today. I have seen dozens of people ruin their lives because they listened to Satan and thought they were listening to Jesus. Churches have been divided. Marriages have dissolved. Families have been torn apart. And Christianity has been mocked and ridiculed because of the acts of His followers who failed to use the discernment He made available to them.

What is discernment? It's the ability to distinguish between what God wants you to do and what you want you to do. It's the ability to clearly distinguish the voice of God from the voice of the enemy. Discernment is the ability to distinguish between a physiological sickness and a demonic attack, between a false prophet and a prophet of God. The apostle John told us to "test the spirits to see whether they are from God" (1 John 4:1). This doesn't mean that you have to ask God whether you should pray for someone. As I've said before, if someone is sick, I pray for the person. I don't feel that I have to wait until God says, *I want you to pray for that person,* because He has already told me to go out and heal the sick, raise the dead, cast out demons, etc.

Yet there are plenty of times when I have to stop and ask, *Lord, is this You or the enemy?* Or I ask, *God, show me what's going on here and the best approach to handle it.*

The Importance of Discernment

There's a story in chapter 13 of the book of 1 Kings that shows the importance of discernment. The story involves a man of God who was sent from Judah to Bethel to prophesy against the evil practices of King Jeroboam. The Bible doesn't even tell us the prophet's name, just that he was a "man of God." When God sent the man on his journey, He told him to return home immediately after giving his message, and He also commanded him not to eat or drink until he had completed his mission.

Clearly, the man of God had a great anointing on him. When he prophesied against the king, Jeroboam pointed at him and shouted for his guards to seize him. Immediately, the king's arm shriveled up and he could not pull it back into his body. At the same time, the altar split apart and the ashes that were on it fell to the ground, just as the man of God had said would happen. When the king saw all of this,

> Then the king said to the man of God, "Intercede with the LORD your God and pray for me that my hand may be restored." So the man of God interceded with the LORD, and the king's hand was restored and became as it was before.
>
> Verse 6

Wow, these were some pretty crazy miracles! So far, so good. Grateful to have his arm restored and obviously realizing that he was in the presence of a true prophet, the king invited the man to come home with him for a meal. He also offered him a gift.

Understand that this wasn't going to be an ordinary meal. This was at a king's table. And Jeroboam ate like a king every day! There was going to be as much food as at the best buffet in Las Vegas, and it was going to be of much better quality. And a gift, too? What might that be? A bag of gold? A brand-new, top-of-the-line chariot with a couple of white stallions to pull it? It certainly wasn't likely to be something from the 99-cent store.

You bet it was tempting, yet the prophet didn't bat an eye:

> But the man of God answered the king, "Even if you were to give me half your possessions, I would not go with you, nor would I eat bread or drink water here. For I was commanded by the word of the LORD: 'You must not eat bread or drink water or return by the way you came.'" So he took another road and did not return by the way he had come to Bethel.
>
> Verses 8–10

But that wasn't the end of the story. Seems there was a "certain old prophet" living in Bethel (verse 11) who found out about what had happened. Even in that day, word spread fast. The old man heard about what the younger prophet had done that day, and he decided to saddle up his donkey and chase after him. It's hard to blame him. Here he was, living in a land that was falling away from God and becoming increasingly corrupt. How he longed to have a conversation with someone else who loved and served the living God, as he did. The Bible says that he found the man of God sitting under an oak tree and asked him to come to his house for a meal.

Once again, the younger prophet explained that the Lord had told him not to stop for a meal. But the older prophet didn't take no for an answer:

> The old prophet answered, "I too am a prophet, as you are. And an angel said to me by the word of the LORD: 'Bring him back with you to your house so that he may eat bread and drink water.'" (But he was lying to him.) So the man of God returned with him and ate and drank in his house.
>
> Verses 18–19

Sadly, the younger prophet didn't even think of taking the time to seek the Lord to find out if the older man was really telling the truth. He did not show an ounce of discernment, and he paid the price on the way home:

> As he went on his way, a lion met him on the road and killed him, and his body was left lying on the road, with both the donkey and the lion standing beside it. Some people who passed by saw the body lying there, with the lion standing beside the body, and they went and reported it in the city where the old prophet lived.
>
> When the prophet who had brought him back from his journey heard of it, he said, "It is the man of God who defied the word of the LORD. The LORD has given him over to

the lion, which has mauled him and killed him, as the word of the LORD had warned him."

Verses 24–26

Moral of the story: Listen to God, not to man. And even if a man tells you that he's passing on a message from God, make sure you check it out for yourself. I have really had to learn this the hard way in my life and ministry. Again, the key is to be open-minded, but not gullible, to be discerning, but not critical.

There's another story a few chapters later about a couple of kings who came to ruin because they chose to listen to false prophets. Chapter 22 of 1 Kings tells us that the kings of Judah and Israel, Jehoshaphat and Ahab, were planning to go to war together. As he made plans for the battle, Ahab called in his prophets and asked them if he would have success in the battle. There were four hundred of them, and their verdict was unanimous. They all prophesied a lopsided victory. One of them even fashioned a pair of iron horns and ran around with them, saying, "This is what the LORD says: 'With these you will gore the Arameans until they are destroyed'" (verse 11).

Pretty dramatic stuff. I can just picture the four hundred prophets shouting to be heard over each other and whipping each other into a frenzy of patriotic fervor. But the truth is that they weren't really prophets. They were company men who told their king what he wanted to hear.

Still, Jehoshaphat, the king of Judah, wasn't satisfied. He knew that Ahab had drifted away from the Lord and had served the ancient Canaanite god Baal. What's more, he had surrounded himself with charlatans and scoundrels. Jehoshaphat wanted to inquire of someone who was a true prophet of God.

Ahab remembered that there was a man named Micaiah who was a faithful prophet of God—"but I hate him because he never prophesies anything good about me" (verse 8).

Despite his friend's objections, Jehoshaphat insisted that they hear from Micaiah, so the prophet was brought before the kings as they sat on their thrones, dressed in their royal splendor. Surely, Micaiah was intimidated. The pressure to go along with what the other "prophets" were saying must have been incredible. In fact, the Bible says that the messenger who went to summon Micaiah into the king's presence told him, "Look, the other prophets without exception are predicting success for the king. Let your word agree with theirs, and speak favorably" (verse 13).

Micaiah replied, "As surely as the LORD lives, I can tell him only what the LORD tells me" (verse 14).

At first, Micaiah did as he had been asked. He told the kings to go into battle and that the Lord would give them the victory—but his voice was dripping with sarcasm. The kings didn't appreciate it and insisted that he tell them the truth. So he did. If they went into battle, they would suffer a crushing defeat. Ahab himself would die in battle.

The other prophets were incensed. The man with the iron horns came up and slapped Micaiah in the face and demanded, "Which way did the spirit from the LORD go when he went from me to speak to you?" (verse 24).

Ahab also reacted predictably. He not only ignored Micaiah's words, but also had him thrown in prison. As the story goes on, the forces of Judah and Israel suffered a crushing defeat:

> So the king of Israel and Jehoshaphat king of Judah went up to Ramoth Gilead. The king of Israel said to Jehoshaphat, "I will enter the battle in disguise, but you wear your royal robes." So the king of Israel disguised himself and went into battle.
>
> Now the king of Aram had ordered his thirty-two chariot commanders, "Do not fight with anyone, small or great, except the king of Israel." When the chariot commanders saw Jehoshaphat, they thought, "Surely this is the king of Israel."

So they turned to attack him, but when Jehoshaphat cried out, the chariot commanders saw that he was not the king of Israel and stopped pursuing him.

But someone drew his bow at random and hit the king of Israel between the sections of his armor. The king told his chariot driver, "Wheel around and get me out of the fighting. I've been wounded." All day long the battle raged, and the king was propped up in his chariot facing the Arameans. The blood from his wound ran onto the floor of the chariot, and that evening he died.

Verses 29–35

Both of these stories from 1 Kings show that God expects us to do everything we can to follow the word that He has given us. If you're not sure you've heard Him properly, just ask Him to tell you. As the book of James says, "If any of you lacks wisdom, you should ask God, who gives generously to all without finding fault, and it will be given to you" (James 1:5).

Staying Rooted

Of course, it's also vitally important to remain rooted in Jesus. Remember what He told His apostles on the night of His betrayal and arrest:

I am the true vine, and my Father is the gardener. . . . Remain in me, as I also remain in you. No branch can bear fruit by itself; it must remain in the vine. Neither can you bear fruit unless you remain in me.

I am the vine; you are the branches. If you remain in me and I in you, you will bear much fruit; apart from me you can do nothing. If you do not remain in me, you are like a branch that is thrown away and withers; such branches are picked up, thrown into the fire and burned. If you remain in me and my words remain in you, ask whatever you wish, and it will be done for you. This is to my Father's glory, that you bear much fruit, showing yourselves to be my disciples.

John 15:1–8

Power flows through us only as we remember our identity is in Jesus. He is our only source of power and life. If we ever forget that, we've lost.

I can think of so many reasons why people start mistaking other voices, even their own, for the voice of Jesus. It happens because they get sucked into pride and start thinking that their success is their own. I don't have to worry about that. If I ever start thinking *I'm Big Time*, Angie brings me back to reality in a flash. You don't know how grateful I am that she has a solid head on her shoulders!

Some people start thinking that God is going to bless them whatever they do. That's why Jim Bakker, who was once one of the most popular evangelists on television, wound up in prison. It's why powerful men of God like my father have fallen into sexual sin.

I tell you, my dad loved the Lord. He spent his whole life trying to build God's Kingdom. He took people in off the streets so he could tell them about Jesus. When I was a child, my father got us out of bed at five every morning so we could pray together. I thank God every day that my parents raised me to know the Lord. And yet, my dad got involved in sexual sin that destroyed his ministry, alienated his family and very nearly cost him his soul. Everything I'm doing today was my father's dream. I'm literally living his dream.

Stay connected to the Vine! Pay attention. Listen carefully. Only then will you know the reality of what Jesus speaks of in the tenth chapter of John:

The one who enters by the gate is the shepherd of the sheep. The gatekeeper opens the gate for him, and the sheep listen to his voice. He calls his own sheep by name and leads them out. When he has brought out all his own, he goes on ahead of them, and his sheep follow him because they know his voice. But they will never follow a stranger; in fact, they will run away from him because they do not recognize a stranger's voice.

Verses 2–5

YOUR ACTIVATION GUIDE

- ► How often does God speak to you? How do you distinguish His voice from the other voices vying for your attention?

- ► Have you ever been mistaken about hearing God's voice? If so, what happened in that situation? What have you done, or what will you do in the future, to avoid making the same mistake again?

- ► In this chapter, we talked about being discerning without being critical, and being open-minded without being gullible. What does this mean to you? Some people seem to accept everything they hear, while others disregard everything. How can we avoid these extremes?

- ► What did Jesus mean when He told us to remain in Him? How do you do this?

- ► There are many stories in the Old Testament of kings who served God faithfully for years and then were seduced into idol worship and sin. You may want to study the stories of Solomon, Jehoshaphat or Josiah. What lesson can we learn from these kings?

9

What to Do When Little Luci Fights Back

When the devil had finished all this tempting, he left
him until a more opportune time.

Luke 4:13

Have you ever seen one of those movies where the bad
guy refuses to die? Every time you think he's dead, he
jumps back up and causes more havoc—especially at the end
of the movie, when you're just sure he's been defeated once
and for all.

I know what you're thinking: *Yeah, Robby, I've seen that once
or twice—or maybe a couple hundred times.*

I know that story is kind of a cliché with Hollywood. But
filmmakers keep using it because it works so well. Besides,
it has its basis in reality. Our old enemy, Satan, is the origi-
nal "monster who would not die." And even though he was

totally defeated by Jesus' resurrection, he still refuses to go away quietly.

As we've already seen, the book of James tells us that if we resist the devil, he will flee from us. But when he does flee, you can be pretty sure that he's only on the run until he can figure out another way to get to you. We have to keep resisting and being on our guard, until he just doesn't have anything left to hit us with.

As you probably recognized, the passage of Scripture I used at the start of this chapter came from the Bible's account of the temptation of Christ. I broke down this teaching in my book *Identity Thief* more, but after Jesus was baptized by John the Baptist, the Holy Spirit led Him into the wilderness. There, Satan tempted Him in several different ways. Each time, Jesus replied by quoting Scripture. Finally, the devil gave up and went away. But as Luke makes clear, he was only going away until "a more opportune time" came along.

Even when it seems that God is blessing us and the devil is being pushed around like he's nothing but a wimp, we have to stay alert. He keeps coming back for more.

In chapter 5, I told you about my experience in England last year, where I saw a young man named Matt who was supernaturally raised from the dead. There were multiple witnesses, including a medical doctor, and they agreed that they had seen Matt come back from death. For the next few days, the pastor of the little church was telling everyone about the miracle that had taken place there. I know, because I was there and I heard him.

Then Satan decided it was time to fight back.

Now, there were somewhere around eighty people remaining in the church's sanctuary that night when Matt died. We were quickly surrounded by a group of eight to ten people who gathered to offer their assistance and to join me in praying for him. Behind these, another ten or fifteen people were close enough to see what was going on. All the people I've been able to talk to have said they watched Matt come back from the dead after we prayed. But, obviously, there were many in the room who were not able to see what was happening.

When word began to get around town about what had happened in their church, some of the parishioners were upset. They didn't like it that their place of worship had become embroiled in a controversy, and I suppose they feared that people might think they were "fanatics," or laugh at them for being "holy rollers." They began pressuring the pastor and others who were there to distance themselves from affirming that Matt's "resurrection" had ever taken place.

To his credit, the pastor would not deny that the event had happened. But bowing to public pressure, he was no longer willing to speak about it publicly.

If I hadn't seen for myself how Satan could stir folks up, it would have surprised me that people became so angry about something they really knew nothing about. They weren't there, so how could they be so sure that the accounts of Matt's miracle were erroneous?

As you might expect, it didn't take long before there were many online reports attacking me as a fake and a charlatan. They're still out there for anyone who wants to read them. As it was written about Jesus' baptism when the Father spoke from heaven, some heard God's voice, while others only heard thunder.

Of course, it hurts when I am accused of being a liar who doesn't really care about anything but money. But I understand two things that make it easier for me to let it go:

1. The attacks are not really aimed at me, but at the Lord I serve.
2. The attacks have come because Satan is angry—and it makes me feel good to know God used me to do something that made him mad.

177

Little Luci Can't Win

Jesus has comforting words for anyone who is suffering because of their service to Him. He said,

> Blessed are you when people insult you, persecute you and falsely say all kinds of evil against you because of me. Rejoice and be glad, because great is your reward in heaven, for in the same way they persecuted the prophets who were before you.
>
> Matthew 5:11–12

And Peter writes,

> Who is going to harm you if you are eager to do good? But even if you should suffer for what is right, you are blessed. 'Do not fear their threats; do not be frightened.' . . . For it is better, if it is God's will, to suffer for doing good than for doing evil.
>
> 1 Peter 3:13–14, 17

There are some important things to remember whenever the devil is seeking to discredit you or comes after you in some way because you have been doing the things that Jesus did. First, Satan may win a battle or two, but he can't possibly win the war. Second, Satan's attempts to fight you will bring God more glory. Third, don't listen to the devil. And fourth, the devil may be your "friend"! Yes, I know that last one sounds heretical, so I'll explain it a little more. In fact, let's take a closer look at each of these important things.

1. Satan may win a battle or two, but he can't possibly win the war.

Sure, the devil has won a few battles. One of these came in the Garden of Eden, where he seduced Adam and Eve into eating the only fruit that God had told them to avoid. That was a major victory because it tainted the whole earth with sin. But that wasn't the final battle. From the beginning, God had a plan to defeat the devil, and He carried it out when Jesus paid the price for our sins through His crucifixion, burial and resurrection.

Satan also won a battle when Jesus went to the cross—or at least he thought he did. But that victory was short-lived. About three days, to be exact. And, by the way, anyone who thinks that it's okay to serve Satan should take a look at the way Jesus died. If ever the devil showed his true colors, it was in the hate and fury he unleashed on Jesus. He wasn't content to kill Jesus. He wanted our Lord to suffer. He was delighted when the soldiers mocked Jesus, slapped and hit Him, and pushed a crown of thorns onto His head until the blood ran down. I can imagine him laughing when our Lord suffered the pain of the flogging that almost killed Him—and when the nails were driven into His hands and feet.

Don't ever underestimate Satan's hatred, anger and fury. But don't ever overestimate his power. He can't do anything that God hasn't prepared us to deal with. Like the honeybee, he may sting you, but in the process, he'll hurt himself a lot more than he is able to hurt you.

I recently came across a news story that brought to mind one of the most devious plans Satan has devised to fight God—namely, communism. During the twentieth century, Communism was the devil's primary weapon in his attempt to wipe Christianity off the face of the earth. As Communism spread across the planet, believers were tortured and imprisoned, churches were padlocked or razed, Bibles were confiscated and forbidden. Communist authorities made it illegal for people to share their faith, even with their own children. Belief in God was ridiculed in public schools and by government leaders. Chairman Mao declared that Christianity would be extinct in China by the end of the 1970s.

This definitely has not happened. In fact, the headline on the article I'm talking about declares, "China on course to become 'world's most Christian nation' within 15 years."[1] The writer goes on to say, "The number of Christians in Communist China is growing so steadily that by 2030 it could have more churchgoers than America."

The story, which appeared in *The Telegraph* in the United Kingdom, continues, "Officially, the People's Republic of China is an atheist country but that is changing fast as many of its 1.3 billion citizens seek meaning and spiritual comfort that neither communism nor capitalism seem to have supplied."

In 1976, the death of Chairman Mao signaled the end of the Cultural Revolution. Since then, churches began reopening and Christian congregations skyrocketed. Fewer than four decades later, some are saying China is now poised to become not only the world's number one economy, but also its most numerous Christian nation. The article goes on:

"By my calculations China is destined to become the largest Christian country in the world very soon," said Fenggang Yang, a professor of sociology at Purdue University and author of Religion in China: Survival and Revival under Communist Rule. . . .

China's Protestant community, which had just one million members in 1949, has already overtaken those of countries more commonly associated with an evangelical boom. In 2010 there were more than 58 million Protestants in China. . . .

Prof Yang, a leading expert on religion in China, believes that number will swell to around 160 million by 2025. That would likely put China ahead even of the United States, which had around 159 million Protestants in 2010 but whose congregations are in decline. . . .

"Mao thought he could eliminate religion. He thought he had accomplished this," Prof Yang said. "It's ironic—they didn't. They actually failed completely."

I keep photos in my phone of persecuted believers who have suffered horrific torture or even death (some are graphic), so that I always remember these heroes of the faith, who will be the most celebrated ones in heaven. This book is dedicated to them.

So much for the devil, who really gave everything he had to destroy the Church in China. In his attempt to eradicate Christianity in China, Satan instead produced some of the strongest, most courageous Christians of our times.

My dear friend Marilyn Hickey gave me a book by Zhang Rongliang in which he tells his story, *I Stand with Christ: The Courageous Life of a Chinese Christian*. Another Chinese Christian I greatly respect is Brother Yun, who wrote *The Heavenly Man: The Remarkable True Story of Chinese Christian Brother Yun*.

The Church in China has survived because in the midst of incredible suffering, the Chinese Christians have seen wonderful miracles and healings. The Chinese Church has even issued a statement saying that its people reject the teaching that the age of miracles has passed.[2] They believe in miracles because they have seen so many of them. Yet the persecution these Christians have suffered has been unimaginable, especially to those of us who live in the comfort of the United States. Rongliang writes of his ordeal at the hands of Chinese authorities. In prison, they hung a special sign around his neck. Its wording ordered the other prisoners to beat him:

It said, "Beat Zhang Rongliang, who opposes the revolution."
. . . I dragged myself through the streets inside the camp as people yelled at me, spit on me, kicked me and threw things at me. I couldn't stop because that would have meant certain death. The only way I could survive was to keep on moving through the mob, no matter how much it hurt. My hands were black from the dirt and mud, and my face was red with blood. The pain was indescribable. . . .

We were beaten at least three times every day, and every room was filled with terror. I could hear the cries of people calling out for their parents. I could hear men screaming for their mothers. People yelled, "Stop" and "Help" over and over, but no one came to help. . . . More than anything else, I heard people crying out to God.[3]

Rongliang goes on for pages, eloquently describing the horrors he suffered. When things reached their lowest point, when he felt that he couldn't go on, a fellow prisoner who was a Muslim came to him and said, "I saw what they did to you today." . . . "I saw them tie you up to the tree, and . . . I saw everything. Zhang? Do you think I can believe in your God? . . . I saw you today, Zhang, and I believe that you serve the one true God."

Rongliang told him, "All you have to do is believe in Jesus. Call upon Him and you will be saved." He writes, "In the darkness of that furnace-like room, I heard him cry out to Jesus that night. My strength was renewed."[4]

In *The Heavenly Man*, Brother Yun writes,

They spread my hands and feet and held me down on the bed. Then they separated my fingers and held them palm-down on a wooden board. The doctor took a large needle, labeled number 6, from his bag. Starting with my left thumb, he jabbed the needle under my fingernails one at a time.

I can't describe how I felt. It was the most excruciating agony I've ever experienced. Intense pain shot through my body. I couldn't help but cry out. . . . By the time the doctor reached my middle finger the Lord mercifully allowed me to faint and not feel the pain being inflicted on me.[5]

Brother Yun's time in prison was horrific. He was beaten again and again, placed in solitary confinement, and tortured by other prisoners, whom the authorities encouraged to abuse him. At one point, when he was too sick to defend himself or even stand up, they took turns urinating on him. But although he suffered terribly, there were many times when God protected him and saved his life. Through his teaching and preaching in prison, many of his fellow prisoners became Christians, and others were healed of potentially deadly diseases. And when he was finally released from prison, the Lord used him to do great things in China. He wrote, "On one occasion I was invited to lead special meetings in Wenzhou, Zhejiang Province, great miracles took place. The blind could see, the deaf could hear, and the lame walked."[6] At another meeting in Anhui Province, four people "who were considered demon-possessed by everyone who knew them"[7] were healed.

All this, coming from a nation where its leader declared Christianity would be completely wiped out of China in a few short years. Oh, my friend, do you see? This is the unshakable Kingdom of God!

2. Satan's attempts to fight you will bring God more glory.

When Satan and his demons come against you, stand firm and watch God use the situation to bring glory and honor to Himself.

Everything Satan does eventually backfires on him. If he weren't the devil, I might even feel sorry for him—just a little. This is kind of a silly analogy, but I see Satan as being kind of like Wile E. Coyote in those old Road Runner cartoons. Remember how Wile E. Coyote was constantly trying to catch the Road Runner, using all these weapons from the Acme Company? He shot missiles, but they came back and blew up in his face. He painted a realistic-looking tunnel on the side of a canyon wall so his prey would smash into it. Instead, the Road Runner ran right through as if it were a real tunnel. But when the poor coyote tried to do the same thing—*smash!* He hit so hard that he had to be scraped off the tunnel wall. And so it went for the poor canine.

Now, please don't get upset with me. I'm not comparing a cartoon with something that is very real and very serious. It's just that whenever Satan devises a plan to harm us, God turns it around and it explodes in his face. There are some things in this world that are never going to change. Wile E. Coyote is never going to catch the Road Runner. Charlie Brown is never going to kick that football. And Satan is never, ever going to get the upper hand on God or His people.

For example, when Satan put it into men's hearts to crucify Jesus Christ, he thought he had destroyed God's plan to save mankind and thereby won control of the universe. He didn't understand that Christ was laying down His life to pay the penalty for our sins. Nor did he know that Jesus would walk out of the tomb three days later, forever glorified. When Satan's plan to destroy Jesus was about to be carried out, Jesus said, "Now the Son of Man is glorified and God is glorified in him" (John 13:31).

As another example, I believe there was spiritual warfare taking place when Lazarus died. After all, Lazarus and his two sisters, Mary and Martha, were three of Jesus' closest friends. If one of them died, Jesus would have been discredited in some people's eyes. They would have gone around whispering that Jesus couldn't really be the Messiah, and that all those stories they'd heard about Him healing the sick must not be true. After all, He couldn't even help this man who was so important to him. Satan certainly thought he had won a big battle there, but Jesus said, "This sickness will not end in death. No, it is for God's glory so that God's Son may be glorified through it" (John 11:4). Then He raised Lazarus from the dead.

One more biblical example: The book of Esther tells of Haman, a wicked man who plotted to destroy the Jews, and who even went so far as to build some gallows. As I'm sure you know, it was not the Jews, but rather Haman himself who was hanged there (see Esther 7).

God will also use Satan's attacks against you for His own glory, and that's just what He's doing through the negative reports about what happened in England on March 9, 2015, with raising Matt from the dead. Because of the reports, more people are hearing about it than otherwise would have. And even though they are hearing the story from a negative point of view, God is able to use that to open people's eyes to what He is doing on this earth. I have had hundreds of messages and emails from people who have written me saying, "I read your story because an atheist friend posted it, mocking it. But as I read it, it touched me, and I believe it happened." Others have told me that since they read the story, they have been taking advantage of every opportunity to pray for the dead to be raised.

The apostle Paul wrote that some people were preaching the Gospel for wrong motives. They were talking about Christ because they thought it was a way to make money for themselves. But whatever their motives were, Christ was being preached, and that made Paul rejoice. We, too, should rejoice when Satan comes against us, knowing that God will be glorified.

3. Don't listen to the devil.

Have you ever noticed that whenever you have a mountain-top experience with God, Satan comes running to try to steal your joy? An acquaintance told me that this is what happened to her right after she attended an exciting conference where she experienced going to the ground under God's power for the first time. She went home full of power and passion, totally excited about what God was doing in her life. But over the next few days, as Satan began to whisper in her ear, she slid into depression. She began to doubt her salvation. She said later that she even questioned God's existence. Thankfully, she had Christian friends who rallied around her, prayed for her and reminded her that she didn't have to listen to Satan's lies. The depression and doubts lifted and have never returned.

I recently prayed for a woman who had several tumors on her neck. As we prayed together, the tumors completely shriveled up and disappeared. I could hardly believe it when one of the first things she said to me after receiving her healing was, "They're gone now, but I won't be surprised if they come back."

Nooooo! We can't allow words like that to come out of our mouths. We can't pay the slightest attention to such thoughts. They weaken us and make us susceptible to Satan's attacks. Remember that he is a liar and the father of lies.

So often after people have seen a miracle, Satan tries to convince them that they didn't really see what they thought they did. A friend of mine was in a bad part of town after dark, and he couldn't get his car started. He didn't know what to do, so he laid hands on the car and prayed that it would start. It did.

The next day he took it to a mechanic, who diagnosed a faulty starter. Without knowing what had happened the night before, the mechanic said, "Sometimes, if you'll rock your car a little bit, the starter will go back into place and the car will start right up."

So it wasn't really a miracle after all, right? Yet it seems to me that it was a miracle no matter what really happened. My friend had no idea that rocking the car might cause it to start.

And he didn't rock the car. This "natural explanation" didn't negate God's intervention.

Why am I telling you this story?

Because you can be sure that the devil and his hordes are going to do everything within their power to make you think that you are a failure and that your prayers are not working. You may pray for someone and see that person's tumors disappear before your eyes, but Satan will try to find a way to convince you that it was just your imagination getting the best of you, or that there was a perfectly natural explanation.

Don't let him fool you, and don't let him stop you from using the power God has placed within you. There is absolutely nothing you can't do!

When the devil comes against you, step out, taking more risk, and punch him in the throat! How do you do that? Do the opposite of the discouraging thought or feeling he puts in you. Let him know that you're not afraid of him, because you have the power of the Holy Spirit within you!

You may not feel as though you're capable of fighting back. You may not feel as though you have enough faith in you to do that. But you know what? Faith is not a feeling. Some of the greatest answers to prayer I have ever seen came when I didn't feel as if I had an ounce of faith in me. God meant what He said when He told Paul, "My power is made perfect in weakness" (2 Corinthians 12:9).

I can't quote any Scripture to support me in this, but I've come to believe that desperation brings more Kingdom activity. In other words, when I'm more desperate for God to move than I am worried about being embarrassed or afraid of what the devil will do, that's when I see God move!

So again, step out! Even if you don't feel that you have any faith, step out. God has filled you with power to break the chains of darkness and bring liberty to people. All you need to do is unleash it.

Every time the devil mocks me and tells me that I'm a failure, I say, "You're right, I fail sometimes. So I may be a failure, but I'm not a quitter!"

Please, don't let Satan and his demons mess with your mind. And don't let him take you on a guilt trip. Satan is a liar and the father of lies; don't listen to anything he says.

Satan will tell you that you are a sinner.

But God says, "Therefore, there is now no condemnation for those who are in Christ Jesus" (Romans 8:1).

Satan will tell you that you are weak and powerless.

But God tells us that we are "more than conquerors through him who loved us" (Romans 8:37).

Satan will tell you that you are nothing but a "dirt clod," a creature made of dust, and destined to return to dust.

But God says that you are created in His image (see Genesis 1:27).

Satan says that you are a disappointment.

But God says, "Well done, good and faithful servant! You have been faithful with a few things; I will put you in charge of many things. Come and share your master's happiness!'" (Matthew 25:21).

Satan says that you are a failure.

But when God looks at you, He sees a winner covered with the righteousness of His Son.

Satan says that your death will be the end of your existence.

But God says you are destined to reign with Him forever (see 2 Timothy 2:12; Revelation 5:9–10).

4. The devil may be your "friend"!

No, that's not a typo. I didn't really mean "fiend." I'd better hurry up and explain what I did mean, however, before someone accuses me of being a heretic. Of course, the devil doesn't want to be our friend. He wants to destroy us body and soul. Instead, he often makes us stronger.

Think about what happens when you go to the gym. According to Dr. William B. Salt,

> You build muscle through resistance training. Scientific studies confirm that resistance training—started at any age—counteracts age-related loss of muscle mass, improves strength and converts fat to muscle. Resistance training improves your ability to perform the activities of life and reduces your injury potential.[8]

Do yourself a favor and start thinking of the devil's attacks as resistance training. I know it's not easy. It's like learning to eat vegetables like celery. You don't eat it because you like it (at least I don't). You eat it because it's good for you. (And if you're a person who loves celery, congratulations on being unique!)

I've talked about this before, but Matthew, Mark and Luke all tell us that Jesus was led into the wilderness by the Holy Spirit after He was baptized, where He was tempted by the devil. The Holy Spirit didn't lead Jesus to run the other way from the devil. Instead, the Spirit led Him directly into a confrontation with Satan. Why was this? Because being tempted by the devil was all part of Jesus' resistance training for His earthly ministry.

Does that mean the Holy Spirit and the devil were on the same side? No, of course not. Satan's intention wasn't to strengthen Jesus, but to destroy Him. But, as our heavenly Father often does, He turned Satan's evil intentions against him and used them for good. How like God! He does that sort of thing so often. Remember what Joseph said to his brothers who had sold him into slavery? "You intended to harm me, but God intended it for good to accomplish what is now being done, the saving of many lives" (Genesis 50:20).

In the same way, Satan meant his temptation of Christ for evil, but God used it for good. And Luke 4:14 reports that after the devil tempted him, "Jesus returned to Galilee in the power of the Spirit."

Not long ago, I traveled to Armenia to meet with some Christian leaders from Iran, where it's a major crime for anyone to convert from Islam. We were just a stone's throw away from Iran. As a matter of fact, it's against the law in Armenia even to tell an Iranian about Jesus. But we were looking for them in the streets so we could pray for them, right under the watchful eye of the secret police. I told them we could discuss healing, deliverance or prophetic ministry, or whatever they most needed to hear. Without hesitation, these Iranian spiritual leaders all said deliverance ministry. They told me that Muslims have no context for how to break demonic power—and that showing power over demons would be a great demonstration of Jesus' power.

One of these leaders was a woman in her twenties who had only been a Christian for six months. But she was a dynamic young lady with a powerful witness, and she had quickly become a leader in the underground Church. Despite her young age, I could see the toll that living under a repressive, anti-Christian government had inflicted on her. The joy of knowing Christ shone in her eyes. But her faced was creased with worry lines, and dark bags circled her eyes.

Strangely—or maybe not so strangely—as soon as we began talking about deliverance, this young woman was hit by a demonic attack. First, she was suddenly gripped by a severe headache. Then, when I began to pray for healing, she also became extremely nauseated.

When I said that this had all the signs of a spiritual attack, one of the other leaders said, "I've always been told that we shouldn't pray for healing because it attracts demons." Then she noticed the shocked look on my face and said, "Demons don't like it when you try to get someone out of their grip. It makes them mad."

"Of course it does," I replied. "All the more reason why you should do it."

I went on to explain that fear of demons should never prevent us from doing something Jesus told us to do—and He clearly told us to heal the sick. I was surprised that any of these people were afraid of demons, seeing as how they had put their lives on the line to serve Christ in a Muslim country. They were some of the bravest people I've ever met, but they had the misperception that demons were powerful entities who were not to be trifled with. They didn't understand that all the weapons the enemy can muster are nothing more than Nerf guns when compared to the power of our Lord!

The Bible asks in Romans 8:31, "If God is for us, who can be against us?" The answer is *nobody!*

Nevertheless, as we continued to pray for healing, the young woman with the upset stomach said, "My nausea and pain are getting worse. I think we should stop."

"No way!" I said. "If you give up now, Satan will bully you. And every time you pray for someone to be healed, he will attack you the same way. You have to keep going. Show him that you're not afraid of him, and that he can't intimidate you."

As we continued to pray, I forbade the demon to manifest. Then I reached out, put my hand on the woman's back and said, "Right now, I bind you, you foul demon, and I pull you out." As I said this, I pulled my hand away from her back and threw it forward, saying, "And I command you to go where the Lord Jesus Christ tells you to go."

Immediately, the woman collapsed onto the couch. "I felt something leave me," she gasped.

"Have you been having night terrors?" I asked.

She looked down and said, "Yes. Every night since I accepted Christ." As tears welled up in her eyes, she said, "I have this immense joy in the daytime, but every night the demons come to me."

That made me furious. I smiled and said, "Well, the demons are gone. Tonight, you're going to have the best night's sleep you've ever had."

Understand that I wasn't prophesying, but speaking in faith. When I saw her the next day, she looked like she was about ten years younger than the day before. She was beaming. The puffy bags under her eyes were gone. No fear showed on her face. The transformation was truly amazing.

"I had the best night's sleep ever," she said. "I didn't have one bad experience. I just feel so filled with energy and strength."

She couldn't wait to get out on the street and start ministering to people, and we saw many people healed and delivered that day.

Remember, there is no power on earth, in heaven or in hell that can stand against the Lord's anointed. And if you are a child of God through faith in Christ, you are His anointed.

YOUR ACTIVATION GUIDE

- ▶ What have you done lately that has made Satan angry? Name as many things as you can think of.
- ▶ How has the devil reacted? Name some specific ways he has tried to fight back.

- How have you handled the devil's attacks? What have you done right, and what have you done wrong? What will you do differently in the future, if anything?
- The Bible says that He who is in you is greater than he who is in the world (see 1 John 4:4). How have you seen this truth manifested in your life?
- Every time Satan tempted Jesus, the Lord responded by quoting Scripture. What Bible verses or portions of Scripture can you use to fight back against the devil?

Stories from the Battlefield

Robby, I was feeling a bit discouraged as I drove to work yesterday. I wondered how much good I was doing through my work as a mentor at a nearby correctional facility. Then, when I got there, I met a new young woman who was assigned to me. I knew nothing about her, but as soon as I sat down, she looked at me and said, "I've met you before. You prayed with me in the lobby several months ago."

I immediately remembered that I met her when she came to visit her boyfriend in jail, and asked her if I could pray for her. She said she didn't need prayer for anything, but she let me pray for her anyway and I gave her a copy of your book *Identity Thief*. I didn't know at the time that she was also battling a serious drug addiction.

So six months later, there she was again, sitting in front of me after I had been assigned to be her mentor while she served time in jail. She and I both sat there stunned, knowing that God had intervened for us and put us together. Wow!

—Darla McElwee

Update: The young lady Darla mentions is now home with her children and is completely free from her drug addiction.

10

What if You Fail?

Jesus said to them, "A prophet is not without honor except in his own town, among his relatives and in his own home." He could not do any miracles there, except lay his hands on a few sick people and heal them. He was amazed at their lack of faith.

Mark 6:4–6

As I've said again and again in this book, I believe that God is ready and willing to answer prayer. There are times when He must say no, but I also believe that if you ask Him why He isn't answering your prayer as you wanted Him to, He'll show you. That certainly has been my experience.

Obviously, there are times when we pray for the sick and they are not healed, or we ask for a desperately needed miracle and it does not come. Sometimes one prayer is not enough. As I said in my book *Do What Jesus Did*, you can't expect to win a war by firing just one bullet. Jesus told us to keep on seeking, asking and knocking. That implies that we may have to pray more than one time before we receive the answer we're looking for.

Before I pray for someone to be healed, I almost always ask the person to tell me what his or her pain level is on a scale of 1 to 10, with ten being excruciating. After I pray, I'll ask, "What's your pain level now?"

Often, the person I'm praying for will tell me that the pain is totally gone. But sometimes, he or she will say something like, "It's about a 5."

After another prayer, it may be a 3 or a 2. We may have to pray a few more times before the healing is complete and the pain is gone completely. But eventually, as Jesus said, "Ask and it will be given to you; seek and you will find; knock and the door will be opened to you. For everyone who asks receives; the one who seeks finds; and to the one who knocks, the door will be opened" (Matthew 7:7–8).

The eighth chapter of Mark tells us about the time Jesus healed a blind man in the city of Bethsaida. The story is kind of a strange one, because it starts off by saying that Jesus took the blind man by the hand, led him out of the village and then spit in his eyes. Can you imagine the man's surprise? I'm sure he was shocked. He could have been offended, but he trusted that Jesus was doing what was best for him. The story goes on:

Jesus asked, "Do you see anything?"

He looked up and said, "I see people; they look like trees walking around."

Once more Jesus put his hands on the man's eyes. Then his eyes were opened, his sight was restored, and he saw everything clearly.

Mark 8:23–25

My point is that it took Jesus two attempts before the man's eyes were completely healed. We're talking about the Lord and Savior of the universe, the One who spoke the universe into being, and it took Him two attempts to restore sight to a blind man.

Jesus is our example in all things, so if He was willing to persevere in prayer for healing, we should be ready to do the same. We can't pray once and then say, "Oh well, I guess it didn't work." We must be willing to pray twice, three times, four times, eight times if necessary. When we're willing to pray until we're exhausted or until we receive what we're asking for, we'll see God's hand at work. And if we pray until we're exhausted and nothing happens, we still can't give up. Keep on knocking, and God will answer.

My hero, John Wimber, said that he prayed for a thousand people before he saw one person healed. After that, God gave many great healings.

My friend Todd White estimates that he prayed for eight hundred folks before one of them was healed.

And in my early days in ministry, I used to joke that I didn't want to pray for anybody, because everybody I prayed for died. It wasn't really that bad, of course. They didn't all die, but they didn't get better either. In *Do What Jesus Did*, I told the story of the first time God answered one of my prayers and healed a man with heart failure who was gravely ill. When the woman who asked me to pray for her father called to tell me that he had been totally healed—that God had even given him a brand-new heart—I didn't believe her. I even told her that I'd have to have proof before I believed her story.

"What?" she asked. "Are you *sure* you're a pastor?" My demand for proof that God had answered my prayer caused her to question my role in the church.

Do You Really Trust God?

Back then, I was shocked if God supernaturally answered one of my prayers. Today, I'm shocked if it doesn't happen. I used to pray for healing, but I never really believed it was going to happen. I didn't know how to activate my faith so that God could use it. The fact is that I didn't really believe God, and believing God is vital.

Remember what happened when Jesus and His disciples were out in a boat on the Sea of Galilee when a terrifying storm came up? The apostles were bailing water like crazy, doing everything within their power to keep the boat from sinking, and here's Jesus sleeping like a baby, without a care in the world. The apostles were scared to death. And even worse, their feelings were hurt. They wanted their Master to get up and help them, and there He lay, totally oblivious to the storm that was raging all around them. (Remember, though, that when Jesus needed them to watch and pray with Him in the Garden of Gethsemane, they all fell asleep!) Finally, they couldn't stand it any longer:

> The disciples went and woke him, saying, "Lord, save us! We're going to drown!"
>
> He replied, "You of little faith, why are you so afraid?" Then he got up and rebuked the winds and the waves, and it was completely calm.
>
> Matthew 8:25–26

Does this mean the disciples themselves could have ended the storm in Jesus' name? That seems like the logical explanation for His words. At the very least, they should have known that their heavenly Father was watching over and protecting them.

One of the points I learn from this story is that if my prayers aren't answered the way I want, it's more likely to be my issue than God's! So when things don't go my way, I don't blame God for it. Instead, I try to figure out how I need to adjust. Or it can be Satan interfering.

Why God Might Say *No*

I stated clearly in *Do What Jesus Did* that I believe when people aren't healed, it is almost always demonic resistance. I still believe that. But does God ever have a reason not to heal? Besides demonic resistance, there may be other reasons why a prayer for healing seems to go unanswered. Even though I believe that may be true, unless God tells me not to pray for healing, I enter into every situation believing that it is His will to heal. I'm convinced that God wants to heal and that He desires for people to be in good health.

The Bible says many times that Jesus healed all the sick who were brought to Him (see, for example, Matthew 8:16; 12:15). In fact, we never see a time when it was not Christ's will to heal someone who came to Him for help. It's true that He did, at first, reject the request of a Canaanite woman whose daughter was tormented by an evil spirit. But this, apparently, was to test her sincerity and her faith (see Matthew 15:21–28).

Some people have suggested to me that it's arrogant to believe that God always wants to heal. My answer is that I believe God desires to heal, because this belief lines up with what I know about who God is. He is compassionate, kind, loving and giving. How can anyone believe that God wants any person to be sick?

Yet one time, I was called to the hospital to pray for a man who was in severe pain. I prayed for him several times, and although the pain diminished, it would not go away. After several prayers, the pain level had dropped to a 2, but it wouldn't go away completely. I finally left his room so he could get some sleep, and I walked away feeling a little defeated and discouraged.

But on my way out of the hospital, I was stopped in the waiting room and asked to pray for two other people. The first was a woman who had serious back pain due to an automobile accident. She was healed instantly. Then I was asked to come pray for a man who was in a coma. As I prayed for him, he opened his eyes and regained consciousness. It was amazing! Several of his family members gave their lives to Christ.

I can believe now that God kept me at the hospital so I could administer His grace and mercy to these two people. If I had left the hospital any earlier than I did, I would have missed those two opportunities.

I was also taking a toll on the devil, however, because the guy I went there for wasn't healed 100 percent. It's important to show the devil that you're not going to give up because he makes it more difficult for you. Let him know that when he hits you, you're going to hit back—hard!

What about a Lack of Faith?

Does a lack of faith hinder your prayers? Well, I believe that God can and does answer the prayers of atheists. As you know, when I'm speaking at a conference or even on the streets, I like to ask if there are any atheists in the audience. If someone raises his or her hand, I invite that person up onstage to help me pray for those who have come for healing. I've seen dozens of powerful miracles brought about by these prayers. Tumors have disappeared. Bent backs have been straightened out. Diseases have been cured. It's so much fun to see the amazed looks on the atheists' faces when they come face-to-face with the power and reality of God. Their mouths fall open. Their eyes bug out. Sometimes, they start shaking as they realize that God is real after all!

God does things like this to reveal Himself. But if that person continues in disbelief despite the experience, I don't think he or she will see many more, if any more, miracles from God's hand.

In fact, I know a lot of believers who suffer from *IF* disease (insufficient faith). God has done miracle after miracle in their lives, and yet every time some sort of crisis comes along, fear takes over. Even though they see all the things God has done to help them in the past, they just can't seem to trust Him for the future. But here's what the book of James says:

> But when you ask, you must believe and not doubt, because the one who doubts is like a wave of the sea, blown and tossed by the wind. That person should not expect to receive anything from the Lord. Such a person is double-minded and unstable in all they do.
>
> James 1:6–8

We've talked before about how Jesus couldn't perform many miracles in Nazareth because of the people's lack of faith. I believe that when we've seen God do so much and yet we still doubt Him, we are cutting off the source of our power.

If you struggle to have faith, I urge you to ask God to cast away your doubts and fears. Be like the man who came to Jesus asking for prayer for his little boy. When Jesus told him that all things are possible for those who believe, he said, "I do believe; help me overcome my unbelief!" (Mark 9:24). His son was healed.

Make a decision that you will believe from this day forward, and see His power flow into your life.

Keep Fighting!

We have to keep fighting until the battle is won. My family and I had an opportunity to go to Italy a couple of years ago. One day while we were there, we took a tour of the Vatican.

I had never been there before, and my boys were all excited about the possibility of seeing the Pope. Every once in a while, one of them would point and yell, "Look! It's the Pope!" But it was always some elderly gentleman who bore no resemblance to the Pope whatsoever.

Then, after that had happened about five times, one of them shouted, "Look!" I turned, expecting to see another elderly man. "It's a boy in a wheelchair!" they said.

Sure enough, a teenage boy in a wheelchair was being pushed along by his mom and dad. As soon as my boys saw him, they wanted to pray for him, so they ran after him. They even began shoving each other away as they ran after him, shouting, "I saw him first!"

"No you didn't. He's mine!"

"Not if I get there before you do!"

They all hustled over and asked the boy and his parents if they could pray for him.

Angie was saying, "Don't hurt the kid in the wheelchair!"

The boy's mother was very nervous about allowing them to pray for him at first, but then she agreed.

They prayed several times for the boy, and guess what happened. He got out of his chair and began to walk around! His mother screamed, and tears ran down her face. The whole family came together in a group hug. They thanked us over and over again.

This young man had the skinniest legs I've ever seen. They seemed too frail to support him, but they were doing a fine job. He seemed unsteady on his feet at first, but the more he walked, the stronger he seemed. A smile spread across his face as he took his first steps in who knows how many years.

My son said, "Jesus was healing you to invite you to a relationship with Him."

The boy told his parents, "Take the wheelchair home. I'm hanging out with these guys the rest of today."

Later that evening, we were in a small café when a blind man came in. This time, I saw him first! I was full of faith because of what had happened with the boy in the wheelchair earlier that day. I rushed over to him, quickly introduced myself and asked if I could pray for him.

"I'd love that!" he said.

I put my hands on his shoulders and prayed, commanding his sight to be restored. Then I told him, "On a scale of 1 to 10, your blindness was at a 10 before. Where is it now?"

"A 10," he replied.

"Do you see anything? Are there any flickers of light?"

"No. Nothing."

I prayed again, but the result was still the same. I took authority over the spirit of blindness in the name of Jesus.

Still nothing.

I asked if I could pray a third time, and the man said no. Then he smiled and asked, "Why don't you let me buy dinner for you and your family?"

"Dinner?" I repeated. "Why would you want to do that?"

"Because I am 65 years old, have been blind my entire life, and you are the first to have the courage to pray for me."

I declined, but I invited him to join us for dinner.

Did God withhold healing, or did the man quit the battle too soon? I have said it before and I will say it again: Healing is war! We are fighting against a real enemy. Even though the man's eyes weren't healed, his heart was touched. And I also know that even when healing doesn't happen, God is glorified. Our obedience brings Him glory.

Selfish Prayers Deplete Power

Selfish prayers deplete the power in your life. The book of James says, "When you ask [in prayer], you do not receive, because you ask with wrong motives, that you may spend what you get on your pleasures" (James 4:3). God is not your Errand Boy. He doesn't seem interested in:

- ► helping you win the lottery
- ► making your favorite team win the Super Bowl, World Series or NBA playoffs
- ► keeping you in the latest Mercedes-Benz
- ► making you the most popular or best-looking person in your school, neighborhood or community
- ► dropping a million dollars out of the sky and into your lap

And the worst thing is, He won't do it for me, either. Or will He?

It's all a matter of motives. God looks at the heart, and only He can tell which prayer is a selfish prayer. Some prayers that might not look selfish to us really are, and some that look selfish may not be. Only God knows. And you can count on the fact that He has a really good sense of humor.

A friend of mine told me about the time more than 25 years ago, when he was standing in line to ride the Jungle Cruise ride at Disney World. It was a hot, humid day and the line wound around and around for what seemed like miles. After standing there for half an hour or so, my friend started to pray that God would make the line move faster.

Nothing happened, so he asked his kids if they wanted to take a break for an ice-cream cone. As he sat there licking at his cone, he started thinking about what a selfish prayer he had been praying. *Lord, please forgive me,* he prayed. *There are so many things to pray about. Children are hungry. People are sick. So many don't even know You.*

As he was silently praying about all these things, he felt a tug on his shirt. He looked up into the face of his six-year-old daughter, who asked, "Dad? Can we go see if the line is better now?"

"Wouldn't you rather ride something else?"

"No. I want to ride the jungle boats."

"Okay. Let's go check it out."

They walked over to the Jungle Cruise ride, prepared for another long wait in the sun.

They were in for a surprise. When they got there, they discovered that there were now two lines. One was jam-packed with people, and the other was completely empty. My friend couldn't believe his eyes, so he stopped someone and asked, "Is this supposed to be a line here?"

"Looks like one to me."

My friend got in that line, walked all the way to the front without making a single stop, and got on board the next boat!

Did God answer a selfish prayer? So it would seem. But He also taught my friend a lesson about His loving, kind nature, and about His power over and concern about even the smallest, most insignificant matters. If something is important to us, it's important to God.

Like I said, this happened over 25 years ago. But it made such a significant impact on us that it will never be forgotten.

Finally, if you ever feel like a failure, remember that you're in very good company. There are few bigger failures in the New Testament than the apostle Peter. Let me give you just a few examples.

Remember what happened to Peter when he tried to walk on water? He and the other apostles were out on the Sea of Galilee in the middle of the night, when Jesus came walking to them across the water. When Peter saw this, he wanted to walk on water, too (see Matthew 14:22–33). When he called out to Jesus, the Lord said, "Come."

Peter threw his legs over the side of the boat and dropped onto the water. He stood there for a moment, his legs shaking beneath him, and then began slowly but surely striding across the waves. Suddenly, the thought came to him that he was doing something no human could do. *I can't do this!* he must have thought, and immediately he began to sink beneath the waves. Just before he sank forever, Jesus reached down, grabbed him and pulled him up.

I can just picture Peter sputtering and gasping for air as he climbed back in the boat, his wet hair dripping like a mop. I'm sure the other disciples must have been covering their faces with their hands, trying to hide their amused laughter. But they couldn't. They had forgotten, for the moment, that Peter was the only one with the courage to try to get out of the boat and walk on the water. And he did! Sometimes we focus way too much on what doesn't happen and miss what does happen.

It was also Peter who told Jesus that he was ready to follow Him anywhere, even to death. Then after Jesus was arrested and put on trial, Peter insisted three times that he didn't even know who Jesus was.

Apparently, Peter wasn't even that great of a fisherman. Remember that on at least one occasion, he had fished all night and hadn't caught a single fish? Not before Jesus came to his aid. He was the kind of guy who acted or spoke first and then thought about it later. If the media had been following Jesus around, they would have loved Peter. He was always shooting off his mouth and would have given them plenty of good sound bites.

And yet, Jesus called Peter a rock and said that "upon this rock I will build my church" (Matthew 16:18 NLT). It fell to Peter to preach the first Gospel sermon on the Day of Pentecost and see thousands of souls come to faith in Christ. Although Paul became the apostle to the Gentiles, it was Peter who opened this door when God sent him to share Jesus with a Roman centurion named Cornelius.

It wouldn't be fair to say that Peter was Jesus' favorite apostle, but obviously it's true that Peter, James and John had a special place in the Lord's heart. The three of them made up His inner circle, and if I had to pick a favorite, I'd certainly pick Peter.

Peter became a man of tremendous courage. He defied the Roman government when he was told to stop teaching in the name of Jesus. He went willingly to prison. He healed the sick and raised the dead in the name of Jesus. He may have started out as something of a failure, but he became one of the greatest men in all of history.

Interestingly enough, when Peter first became a follower of Jesus, his name wasn't even Peter. It was Simon. It was Jesus who gave him the faith and power he needed to become a rock and a great man of God.

Believe me, God can and will do the same thing with us.

When we give Jesus our failures, He will turn them into victories. We can count on it.

YOUR ACTIVATION GUIDE

- ▶ Can you recall the last time you felt as though God didn't answer your prayer the way you wanted Him to? As you look back, can you see some specific reasons why God said no? List some of the good things that resulted from His answer.

- ▶ In this chapter, we discussed several reasons why God may say no to our prayers. What are some other reasons why He may not answer our prayers as we desire?

- ▶ How should we respond when we think God is saying no?

▶ In the Garden of Gethsemane, Jesus prayed that He might be delivered from the cup of suffering that awaited Him. What would have happened if the Father had granted His request? What personal lesson can we learn from this?

▶ What do you think Jesus meant when He told us to seek first the Kingdom of God? How does this change our prayers? How does this change the result of our prayers?

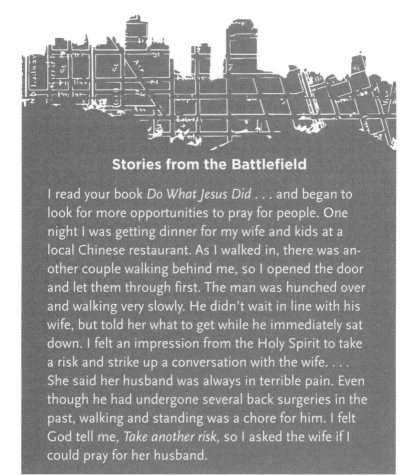

Stories from the Battlefield

I read your book *Do What Jesus Did* . . . and began to look for more opportunities to pray for people. One night I was getting dinner for my wife and kids at a local Chinese restaurant. As I walked in, there was another couple walking behind me, so I opened the door and let them through first. The man was hunched over and walking very slowly. He didn't wait in line with his wife, but told her what to get while he immediately sat down. I felt an impression from the Holy Spirit to take a risk and strike up a conversation with the wife. . . . She said her husband was always in terrible pain. Even though he had undergone several back surgeries in the past, walking and standing was a chore for him. I felt God tell me, *Take another risk*, so I asked the wife if I could pray for her husband.

She looked at me funny because we were both in the middle of getting food, but said, "Well, why don't you ask him?"

I got my food, and on my way out I approached the gentleman and said, "I know this sounds funny, but I was talking with your wife, and I would love to pray for you."

"After looking me up and down a bit to see if I looked too weird, he said, "Okay."

I asked him, "On a scale of 1 to 10, how bad is your pain?"

He replied, "When I'm sitting down, I'm okay, but if I stand up, it's a constant 10."

I thought to myself, *God, what have You gotten me into? I've never prayed for someone with a pain of 10 before.* I began to pray healing over his back and command the pain off him in Jesus' name. As I was praying, I felt God tell me, *Take another risk, and tell him to stand up.*

By now, there were other people in the restaurant watching us, but I did it anyway. I said, "I know this might sound weird, but I want you to stand up and tell me honestly if your pain is the same or if it's any less. Don't lie to me. If it's still a 10, you won't hurt my feelings."

He looked at his wife with a little trepidation, but then started to get up from his seat. He looked at me, looked at his wife, and then looked at me again with a smile and said, "Well, that was pretty easy!"

We both stood there for a second, kind of dazed, before we realized our food was getting cold. He hugged me and I hugged him back, and then I went home praising God and saying, *If this is what divine*

appointments look like, then sign me up! And by the way
. . . my fortune cookie didn't say anything about healing
a guy in Jesus' name that night.

—Steve Goodrich

11

Gaining the Victory in Jesus

But thanks be to God! He gives us the victory through our Lord Jesus Christ.

Therefore, my dear brothers and sisters, stand firm. Let nothing move you. Always give yourselves fully to the work of the Lord, because you know that your labor in the Lord is not in vain.

1 Corinthians 15:57–58

I was in a sit-down coffee shop, along with my son Isaiah, a businessman/friend whom I've been mentoring named Gordon Cowan, and Brian "Head" Welch, lead guitarist and co-founder of the heavy metal band Korn, when God directed my attention to one of the baristas who was taking her break. I sensed that something was wrong with her back, but because we were focused on other things at the moment, I didn't want to distract from the conversation and turn my companions' attention to the fact that I sensed her need for healing.

But Brian turned to me and said, "Jesus is speaking to you about that girl over there, isn't He?"

I nodded, "Yup." Silently thanking God for Brian's sensitivity, I walked over to the young woman. Her name tag told me that her name was Colleen.

"Excuse me," I said. "I'm Robby . . . and Jesus shows me things about people He loves. I think He is showing me that you've been in a car accident that injured your back and your hip."

"That's right," she said, "but how did you know?"

I reminded her that I knew because the Lord had told me.

"Well, it's true," she said. "I was in a car accident and spent months in a wheelchair. I've been in constant pain ever since."

I told her that if she let us pray for her, Jesus would heal her completely right there.

"Sure. I'll try anything that will help me feel better."

It wasn't the most enthusiastic answer I've ever heard, but it was an opening God could and would use. I put my hands on her back and prayed a brief prayer for her healing, while Brian, Isaiah and Gordon looked on and thanked Jesus for His love and power.

As I closed the prayer, a look of astonishment spread across Colleen's face. Surprise quickly gave way to a smile that stretched from ear to ear.

"It doesn't hurt anymore."

"Are you sure? Give it a really good check."

She bent down and touched her toes effortlessly.

"I couldn't do that before."

She stood up and put her arms over her head, stretching as far as she could. "I couldn't do that either! The pain is gone!"

I told her, "Jesus healed your back because He wants a relationship with you."

Her eyes filled with tears, and she said, "I don't know what you mean. I've never been to church, really."

I briefly explained to her what Jesus had done for her through His death, burial and resurrection, and I told her that she could accept Him right then and there if she wanted to.

"Would you mind if my friend Brian here prayed for you to start a relationship with Jesus?" I asked.

"Not at all. I'd love it."

The girl had no clue who Brian was, and he was loving the fact she didn't recognize him—though he had 32,000 fans just down the road waiting for him and the other members of Korn to take the stage at Toyota Stadium in Chicago. What we were doing with this girl is the stuff Brian loves most in life. Brian shared a bit of his testimony and then led her in a beautiful prayer as she surrendered her life to Christ. Brian is a pro at it. He leads dozens of people to Jesus nearly every night after his band's shows.

We all rejoiced as Colleen finished her prayer, and Brian remarked, "I've got to buy her a Bible." He told her that she needed to start reading the Bible, that we were going to run out and buy her one, and that we'd be back as soon as possible.

We went outside, hopped in the car and drove off, looking for a store where we could buy a copy of God's Word. We wound up at Wal-Mart, which we figured would have a lot of Bibles to choose from. We were wrong about that. There was only an easy-to-read Bible in stock, and it had a bright pink cover. It wouldn't do for everyone, but we thought it was perfect for Colleen.

Brian laughed out loud when he saw it. "Oh, this is so Jesus," he said.

By the time we got back to Starbucks, Colleen's grandmother was there. Colleen introduced us and told us that she had called her grandmother and asked her to come down to the store so we could pray for her. The woman had been dealing with some serious health issues for a long time. Now that Colleen had experienced the love and power of Jesus for herself, she wanted the same for her grandmother, whom she loved dearly.

Of course, we were happy to pray for her grandmother, and we rejoiced with her as she experienced the Lord's healing touch and came into His Kingdom.

Korn for Christ

God is putting together an army of righteousness to take His love and His Word into all the world. Some of those who are giving their all to His cause, who would be willing to give their lives for Him if He called them to do so, were fighting on the other side just a few years ago.

Their lives have been changed in an instant, just like the apostle Paul, who was confronted by the resurrected Christ while traveling to Damascus to persecute believers there. One of these is my dear friend Brian Welch from Korn. Brian, who is also known as "Head," is one of the most on-fire Jesus lovers I know. Whenever there is an opportunity to express Jesus, he is most eager to step out in faith.

I want to tell you about Brian, not because he's a famous rock singer, but rather because he is yet another example of what an ordinary person can do when he or she is totally committed to Jesus and totally willing to follow Him anywhere He leads. Brian doesn't have a degree in theology, he didn't grow up in a church, nor does he have thirty years of experience as a follower of the Lord. But Brian loves Jesus and wants the Lord to use Him for His glory—and amazing things happen when he prays.

For ten years beginning in 1993, Brian was a member of one of the world's most successful nu metal bands. Korn sold millions of albums and made millions of dollars. Brian was riding high, but he was also addicted to drugs. By 2003, he had become an addict. He says that he would prepare for tours by stashing as much methamphetamine as possible in vitamin capsules, deodorant containers and his clothes. He also said, "We were only sober for just a couple of hours a day in Korn. Every day."[1]

Korn wasn't exactly "preaching the Gospel" to its millions of fans. CBN News said that Korn's lyrics were "dark, sexually explicit, and disturbing," and quoted the *Chicago Tribune* as calling the members of the band "perverts, psychopaths, and paranoiacs."[2]

Brian said he felt that he was stuck in a trap, and there was no escape:

> You travel, you get to another town, you play a show and you do it again. You try to just be at peace but even a big, huge band like Korn, playing in front of thousands of people, it can get lonely. You feel like you're a trucker and you're traveling with a bunch of truckers. You can't connect with people except for the ones that you're with because the ones you party with after the show, you don't know them and then you're gone.[3]

Early in 2005, a friend gave Brian a Bible, and he began to read it. On February 22 of that year, Korn issued a statement saying that he had left the band, after choosing "the Lord Jesus Christ as his Savior, and will be dedicating his musical pursuits to that end."[4] Brian has told me that he had a revelation of Christ, which convinced him that he could not stay in the lifestyle he had chosen. He was also a single father of a young daughter, and he was concerned about her life and future more than his own.

A week after announcing that he had become a Christian, Brian flew to Israel and was baptized in the Jordan River, along with a number of other members from his church in Bakersfield, California. With God's help, he overcame his addiction to drugs and went to some of the most impoverished areas of India, where he began building orphanages.

Now, when I tell you that Brian overcame his addiction with God's help, I want to explain that he did not join a 12-step program nor go into rehab—although I have seen how God works through programs like Celebrate Recovery and Alcoholics Anonymous, and I praise Him for them. But instead, Brian locked himself into a hotel room and spent hours praying and wrestling with God about his addictions. In many ways his battle was like that of Jacob, recorded in Genesis 32:

> So Jacob was left alone, and a man wrestled with him till daybreak. When the man saw that he could not overpower him, he touched the socket of Jacob's hip so that his hip was wrenched as he wrestled with the man. Then the man said, "Let me go, for it is daybreak."
> But Jacob replied, "I will not let you go unless you bless me."
> The man asked him, "What is your name?"
> "Jacob," he answered.
> Then the man said, "Your name will no longer be Jacob, but Israel, because you have struggled with God and with humans and have overcome."
> Jacob said, "Please tell me your name."
> But he replied, "Why do you ask my name?" Then he blessed him there.
> So Jacob called the place Peniel, saying, "It is because I saw God face to face, and yet my life was spared."
>
> Verses 24–30

By the time Brian Welch walked out of that hotel room, he was completely free of the addictions that had enslaved him for years. As that story illustrates, he is a man of dynamic faith and action.

It's been a privilege for me to get to know Brian and call him friend. He has joined me at many of my conferences, as well as traveling with me to Chile for a mission trip where we ministered to a couple thousand teenagers. I've had the thrill of stepping out and giving prophetic words, doing healing and pushing Brian out to do the same as he shared Jesus at a number of Korn concerts. He never shrinks back from going out into the streets to share the love and power of God.

Never Be Embarrassed

One thing that I greatly admire about Brian is that he is never afraid to put Jesus on display. Being on fire for Jesus means being unwilling to "tone it down" when we're around people who are "too cool" to get excited about Him.

Brian is not embarrassed to talk about Jesus one-on-one with a cashier in a coffee shop, and he's not embarrassed to talk about Jesus in front of hard-core fans at a Korn concert.

Brian has been accused of being "over the top," but I'm convinced that's the way Jesus expects us to be. As He says in the book of Revelation, "I know your deeds, that you are neither cold nor hot. I wish you were either one or the other! So, because you are lukewarm—neither hot nor cold—I am about to spit you out of my mouth" (Revelation 3:15–16).

If we want to see people healed and delivered, we've got to be the same way. We can't wear our Jesus shirt when we're with our Christian friends and then put a jacket over it to hide it when we're with our nonbelieving friends from work or school.

Jesus also talked about this in the book of Luke: "Whoever is ashamed of me and my words, the Son of Man will be ashamed of them when he comes in his glory and in the glory of the Father and of the holy angels" (Luke 9:26).

Back to Korn

After ten years away from Korn, Brian Welch rejoined the group, by mutual agreement. Brian missed playing the music that had been so important to him for years, and the other members of the band said they were willing to let him talk about Jesus. More importantly, he knew that playing with Korn would give him an opportunity to reach many more people for Jesus.

Still, as much as he loves playing his guitar and performing in front of large audiences, telling people about Jesus is what's really important to Brian Welch.

The first time I attended a Korn concert, over thirty thousand people were there. Now, many of you may have a difficult time picturing most of those people sitting in church on Sunday morning. Yet if you want to catch fish, you have to go where the fish are. If you want to bring people into God's Kingdom, you have to go where the lost are.

I have had the privilege of praying for many people at Korn concerts, and I have seen incredible healings take place. Some people make the mistake of thinking that God is confined to the church—that He only shows up where the singing of hymns and lifting of hands is taking place. But the Spirit of God can and does go anywhere where He is welcome and acknowledged.

I can tell you this: Jesus likes showing up and bringing people to Himself at Korn shows. As the Bible says, the Holy Spirit is like the wind, which "blows wherever it pleases" (John 3:8).

On the Road with Korn

Here's how it works when I'm at a Korn concert. While the band is getting ready to come out onstage, I walk through the audience with several other people and hand out about forty wristbands. There's a lot of prayer involved, because it's important that the wristbands are given to those God wants to have them. These forty or so people are then invited to a designated meeting area after the concert for a "Private Meet and Greet" with Brian. He wants to keep the group small, because he desires to look them in the eyes and have a personal connection with them while he shares with them about how Jesus has changed his life.

Once he does that, he asks the group, "How many of you would like to experience God in your life?"

Usually, somewhere between half and two-thirds of the people raise their hands, and if I'm there, he'll ask me if I have any words of knowledge to share. I give words about people who need healing or prayer for other needs. When the Lord responds, as He always does, I let people know that Jesus has given these miracles to show how much He loves them, and that He wants to have a relationship with them. As a result, an amazing number of people have been saved at Korn concerts.

Still, things don't always go smoothly. Even though Brian has made a strong stand for Christ and is known all over the world for his faith, Korn still has millions of fans from the "old days" before Brian's conversion, when just about everything was about drugs, drinking and sex—and a lot of those people are openly contemptuous of God. In some ways, then, a Korn concert could be considered symbolic of the battle between good and evil.

For example, at a concert in Peoria, Illinois, I thought for a moment that I had given one of those wristbands to the wrong guy. He showed up completely drunk for the meeting with Brian, and he kept shouting inappropriate comments—mainly about how he wanted to take Brian out to a strip club and show him a good time. It wasn't exactly the sort of thing you want to be happening when you're trying to tell people about Jesus.

Still, the Lord was there, and He gave me a word of knowledge for one of the other men in attendance. "God has shown me that you're in desperate need of a job," I told him.

"That's right," he agreed. "I've been out of work for over a year. I've looked and looked, but I just can't find anything."

"And there's a problem with your back?"

He nodded and told me that he had hurt his back a couple of years ago, and he'd been in terrible pain ever since.

"How bad is it?" I asked. "Can you touch your toes?"

"Not even close," he said.

"Give it a try. Show me what you can do."

He bent over slightly from his waist, and he was right. He could barely reach his thighs, much less his knees.

I prayed for him and asked him to try again. This time, much to his surprise, he bent all the way over and touched his toes without so much as a wince or grunt. His back pain had vanished, and he began twisting and bending over in different directions to check out his "new" back. Everything worked perfectly.

After that, I announced, "God is showing me that there's someone here with a bad knee. . . ."

"Wait a minute, Robby," Brian said.

I stopped in midsentence, surprised by the interruption.

"This is the next person you need to pray for." He walked over and stood next to "Mr. Strip Club."

"Okay, anybody else?" I said.

But Brian persisted. "He broke his back at a Korn concert eight years ago."

He explained that the young man had been crowd-surfing when he was dropped and fell to the floor, fracturing several bones in his back. It also resulted in multiple bulging disks. Doctors said he was fortunate that he hadn't wound up paralyzed, but he hadn't had a day without severe pain since then. The guy didn't really believe in the power of prayer. In fact, he was an atheist, but that changed when he saw the look on the other man's face after he was prayed for, and watched as he bent over and easily touched his toes. His silly, inebriated grin disappeared as hope grew in him.

The young man later told us that he hadn't been able to tie his shoes ever since his crowd-surfing accident. Herniated disks kept him from bending over and touching his toes. His range of motion was severely restricted.

But after I coached the other guy—the one whose back had just been healed—in praying for him, he was able to do both. One other amazing thing happened that night. He was drunk when the first fellow laid hands on him and began to pray. When we finished, he was completely sober. In other words, he went from falling-down drunk to stone-cold sober in a matter of about thirty seconds. As I often do, I asked him to give me his pain level, on a scale of 1 to 10. When he said his pain was gone, I told him not to be nice to me.

"I'm not being nice to you," he said. "There is no pain."

He began walking around the room, twisting his body in all directions. "I couldn't do this when I came in here tonight," he said. "I haven't done any of this in eight years."

He was rapidly walking around the room with his hands on his hips, bending back and forth so much that I was half afraid he might throw his back out.

I turned to the man whom I had coached to pray for him and said, "Jesus just invited you to a relationship with Him. He just showed you how He wants to use you the rest of your life."

He told me that he wasn't a believer, but now he wanted to be. Both men had just come to see Korn, and they did. But they also met Jesus. They both shook their heads in amazement.

"To think that I was healed and accepted Jesus at a Korn concert!" one said.

We actually have it all on video.

You would think that everyone watching there that night, who all saw such a miraculous healing, would fall to their knees in awe and ask to accept Jesus, but not all of them did. Most responded, but many others stood there like statues, looking on in silence. Some even stomped away outraged.

The best way I can describe it is to say that it was like being at a football game where the quarterback threw a long touchdown pass for the home team and nobody cheered. Jesus had just shown His power and love in a mighty way, yet some people acted as if they hadn't seen anything. Brian, who is usually one of the most energetic and positive guys you'd ever want to meet, was particularly discouraged.

When everyone had gone, he shook his head and asked me, "What's wrong with people? You would think that after seeing Jesus do a miracle like that, they would be falling on their knees and calling out for Jesus to save and heal them. Instead, they just stand there like it's no big deal."

"I know," I agreed. "But I think it's just that we have to wait for people's hearts to catch up with what their eyes have seen. Their eyes have seen His power, but the reality of it hasn't yet sunk down into their hearts."

Sometimes people don't respond immediately, so all we can do is plant the seeds of faith and wait for them to grow. But it's important to remember that, as Jesus taught, even the tiniest seed can grow into a mighty plant "with such big branches that the birds can perch in its shade" (Mark 4:32).

Jesus at the Rock Concert

Are some people offended to think that Jesus would show up at a heavy metal concert? Of course they are. Some Christians will never know how far Jesus will go to become the friend of sinners.

During the three years when He was on this earth in human flesh, Jesus put His own reputation on the line because He often hung out with the seediest types of people. The heavy metal, hip-hop and rap communities of our day probably aren't looked upon much differently than were the prostitutes, tax collectors, Samaritans, drunkards and sinners of Jesus' day.

Respectability was never very high on Jesus' list of priorities. As His followers, we get to be just as worried about our reputations as He was about His. As the great British missionary C. T. Studd wrote,

> Some want to live within the sound of church or chapel bell;
> I want to run a rescue shop within a yard of hell.[5]

Bestselling recording artist Steve Camp wrote his own version of that song in the 1980s, saying that he wanted to run in the shadows a yard from hell's gates because we have to run to the battle. It's a great location, where you and I can do greater things.

YOUR ACTIVATION GUIDE

- ► Has Jesus ever called you to go where you didn't want to go or do what you didn't want to do? What happened?
- ► Do you think Jesus would attend a Korn concert? Why or why not?
- ► Do you believe Brian Welch did the right thing by returning to Korn? Explain your answer.
- ► Where is the strangest place you have ever seen God at work? What happened?
- ► Name some specific instances where Jesus has given you the victory over issues, sickness and/or spiritual darkness.

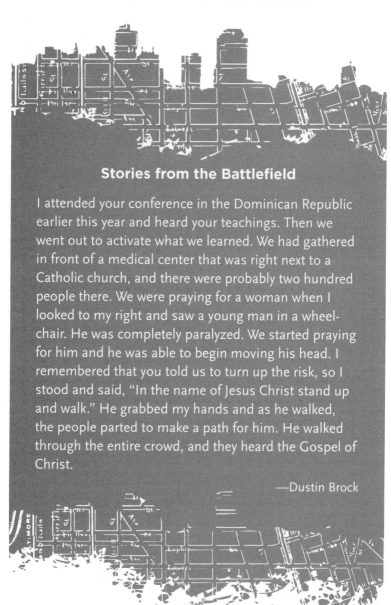

Stories from the Battlefield

I attended your conference in the Dominican Republic earlier this year and heard your teachings. Then we went out to activate what we learned. We had gathered in front of a medical center that was right next to a Catholic church, and there were probably two hundred people there. We were praying for a woman when I looked to my right and saw a young man in a wheelchair. He was completely paralyzed. We started praying for him and he was able to begin moving his head. I remembered that you told us to turn up the risk, so I stood and said, "In the name of Jesus Christ stand up and walk." He grabbed my hands and as he walked, the people parted to make a path for him. He walked through the entire crowd, and they heard the Gospel of Christ.

—Dustin Brock

12

Amazing Things Happen When Atheists Pray

Everyone who calls on the name of the Lord will be saved.

Romans 10:13

In Chile, I was speaking in front of a crowd of seven hundred people, most of them on-fire believers in Jesus. As we were praying for the sick, I called out something I almost always ask: "Are there any atheists in the audience tonight? If you don't believe in God, stand up and let me know."

Usually in a crowd of that size, there are at least four or five people who admit they aren't believers, and maybe three or so who admit to being atheists. On that night, I saw none.

Then I thought, *Wait a minute!* Way in the back, a middle-aged man was standing and waving at me. And in the middle of the auditorium, about ten rows back, a young girl with a sheepish look on her face was also standing and raising her hand. She didn't look as if she wanted to do it, but some of her young friends were urging her to let her lack of faith be known.

"Thank you . . . and you," I said. "Are there any more atheists here?"

Apparently, the answer was no.

"Okay," I said, "both of you who stood up, I want you to come up on the stage with me."

The man immediately sat down, folded his arms across his chest and began shaking his head vigorously. Apparently, he was not willing to fall into my clutches. The young girl began edging her way to the aisle, and slowly walked up the stairs to the stage. Her face told me she wanted to turn and run, but to her credit, she didn't.

She told me that her name was Sofia Vidal and that she was seventeen years old. When I asked her again if she was an atheist, she assured me that she didn't believe in God.

I introduced her to a woman who had come forward because she had a problem with a disk in her back and was in so much pain that she could barely turn her head. I explained to the girl that I wanted her to pray for the woman so that she might be healed.

"But I don't know. . . ."

"Just put your hand on her back . . . gently now . . . and I'll tell you what to say. Please repeat after me. . . ."

The girl did what I said as I led her in a prayer for healing in the name of Jesus. We took authority over the pain and commanded it to leave and never return. We commanded the back to be restored.

After I pray for someone, I always ask, "If you were at a 10 in pain when we started and 0 is no pain, what is your pain level now?" In this case, I didn't have to ask, because I already knew. In the middle of the prayer, the woman started twisting around as if she were watching a workout video. When she came for prayer, she had been moving as if she had a big piece of plywood stuck up the back of her shirt. In other words, she was extremely stiff and walking very, very carefully.

Not anymore. And she had a huge grin on her face. "It's a 2!" I said, "Let's pray again." We commanded the pain to go to a 0, and I asked again.

"It's gone! The pain is gone!" she replied.

Naturally, we rejoiced over the healing. Then I turned to my young helper and asked her, "What do you think of that? You said you don't believe in God, but you saw what just happened."

She shook her head, but I thought she was going to cry. She walked away as we called for others who needed healing.

Later, at the end of the evening, I was sitting in the back praying, signing my books and chatting with people who had questions.

Sofia approached me. Looking angry, she blurted out, "He must be real! But if He is, why didn't He heal my mother?"

"Your mother? What happened to your mother?"

"She died from cancer. About two years ago."

I told her how sorry I was to hear that.

"I prayed so hard for her. But it didn't help. She just got sicker, and then she died. When that happened, I decided I wouldn't believe in God anymore."

"But God didn't let your mother die," I told her.

"He didn't?"

"No. Satan was responsible for your mom's death. God wanted to save her. He was as heartbroken over her death as you were."

I explained that Satan is the one who wants to see us sick and suffering. God wants us healed, but Satan has real authority that God honors. And when the enemy takes the lives of God's followers, God takes them home to heaven. It's vitally important to realize that the death and sickness we experience are not part of God's Kingdom and plan, but rather Satan's. Until God's Kingdom is fully established, the effects of Satan's rule on the earth are in effect.

As we talked, a hard look came into her face.

"Something is making you very angry right now," I said, and she nodded that I was right.

"Can I pray that you'll feel the reality of God's presence?" She agreed, and as I started to pray she began to perspire— a little at first, and then a lot. Sweat was pouring down her face. I knew she was in a spiritual battle, and I asked her, "Can you feel that?"

"Yes," she answered. "I can feel electricity all over, but something is fighting it."

I then bound Satan and commanded him to leave immediately. When I did, she opened her eyes, and it seemed to me that I saw the light come into them. Large tears of joy and relief slowly rolled down her face.

I asked her if she was ready to invite Jesus into her life, and she heartily said, "Yes!"

As we prayed together, Sofia was filled with even more joy. The next day at church she came bouncing up to me, but I barely recognized her. She was glowing and wearing a smile that stretched from ear to ear—a brand-new girl.

Hey, Atheist, Try On My Faith

There are so many important lessons to be learned from an evening like the one I just described. But what I want us to see right now is that God does listen when atheists pray, and He responds. I'm not saying that someone can continue to turn his or her back on God and still expect Him to answer prayer. There are plenty of Scriptures that tell us that God will eventually turn away from the one who turns away from Him.

But God looks at the heart. What I have learned through my years of relationship with Him is that He sees the difference between a heart that has been wounded and one that has been hardened by selfishness and pride.

228

As we've discussed throughout this book, I believe that healings, miracles and other answers to prayer are signs and wonders that God gives to show people that the Gospel message is absolutely true. I will even go so far as to say that I believe God loves to answer the prayers of atheists, especially as they pray in His name for others. I have seen Him do it so many times, and I can't help but believe that it makes the angels laugh when they see atheists' eyes roll back in their heads as the truth overwhelms them.

If you want to see God's power in action, I believe one of the best things you can do is get an atheist to pray. Not one of those angry, hard-baked atheists who still won't believe in God even when he or she sees Jesus coming in power and glory. But if you know any atheists who think they have reasoned away their need for God, or who can't believe because their feelings have been hurt in some way, ask them to pray. And just watch how God responds to them.

I'm sure you've figured out by now that the church Angie and I started in Aurora, Illinois, included a lot of people who came to Jesus out of addiction to drugs or alcohol. More than once, I've had people tell me that they were in desperate trouble—even thinking that they were dying—when they called out to God to save them. They weren't even sure they believed in God, or knew who He was. But Jesus Christ was there, heard their cries and delivered them from the clutches of evil. When they cried out to God, they were atheists. They weren't motivated by faith, but by desperation. God met them in their moment of despair, and now they know, love and serve Him.

Encounter at O'Hare

Angie and I were supposed to fly to London for some meetings there. Due to bad weather, our local flight had to turn back from heading to Chicago and return to Central Illinois

Regional Airport. This meant we had to drive to O'Hare International Airport in Chicago. While we were sitting in the lounge at O'Hare, waiting for news about our flight, we started talking to two other couples who were also waiting. There was an older couple who seemed to be devout Christians, and a middle-aged Jewish couple. In the course of our conversation, the Christian lady said, "I work in a church, and I really enjoy it."

I asked about her job, and after she told me about it, she asked what I do for a living.

I was thrilled to tell her, "I get to equip people all over the world to use the power of the Holy Spirit in healing, deliverance, words of knowledge and God's manifest presence to bring people into a relationship with Jesus."

Her response wasn't quite what I hoped for.

"Oh we believe that God heals," she told me, "but it just isn't that prevalent and shouldn't be pursued."

I smiled and replied, "Well, it may shock you how often it happens. As a matter of fact, I'll have atheists pray for people in the name Jesus and see them get healed." I went on to tell her how many times I have seen atheists come to Jesus in this way.

Her brow wrinkled, and she cocked her head to one side as if she couldn't believe what I'd just said.

"Hang on there a minute, young man," she said. "That's really not appropriate. You shouldn't teach atheists to pray like that."

At this point, the Jewish woman spoke up. "What about Jewish people? Will Jesus use Jewish people to do that?"

"Well, of course," I told her. "After all, Jesus was Jewish."

The Christian lady rebuked me again and said I was confusing these people.

But the Jewish woman shook her head and said, "I'm not confused, I'm intrigued."

I said, "Well, why don't we check it out right now? Do either one of you have pain in the lower part of your back due to degenerating disks? Are you in constant pain?"

The Jewish woman said, "Not me."

Then her husband nodded. "That would be me," he said, "but I've had this issue for over twenty years, and it will never go away."

I smiled and said, "Sir, Jesus is about to heal your back completely right now. He'll do that because He wants you to know how much He loves you and because He's inviting you into a relationship with Him."

The Christian lady didn't like this one bit. "Hold on—this is getting dangerous!" she protested.

The Jewish gentleman disagreed. "No, let's see if this is real." He turned to me. "Go ahead, but it won't work."

"That's right, it won't," agreed the Christian woman.

I asked the man, whom I'll call Michael, to tell me how bad his pain was, using a scale of 1 to 10.

"It's 15 and getting worse," he said.

I asked his wife to lay hands on Michael, and as she repeated after me, I prayed, "Father, I thank You for Your healing power. As a sign to Michael that You love him and are pursuing him, I command this back to be healed right now for Your great glory. Back, be healed for the glory of Jesus Christ right now."

When we finished, I asked Michael if he felt better. He began to twist around in his seat, and then he got up and bent over and touched his toes. He shook his head in surprise and exclaimed, "I'd say it's down to . . . maybe a 1!"

We prayed again, and he told me the pain was completely gone. I knew he was telling the truth, because I could see the relief and joy on his face.

I said, "You see, Jesus just invited you into a relationship with Him by healing you. How would you like to respond?"

He said, "Well, my mind has just been blown," and began to wipe tears from his eyes.

Meanwhile, the Christian couple sat with arms folded, obviously feeling that I had done something horribly wrong. About that time, we were all called to the front desk for the flight.

I grabbed Michael's hand while he was still wiping tears away and said, "I may not see you after this. Will you please remember Jesus' invitation to you?"

"Robby, I will never forget it as long as I live. How could I?" he answered.

Don't get sucked into people's arguments and unbelief. Just put Jesus on display. As my friend Brian Blount says, "He will settle the argument. He is a big God with broad shoulders."

The Power of Prayer

One of the amazing things about prayer is that it changes the one who prays as much as it does the one who is being prayed for. When someone prays, even a nonbeliever, there is an undeniable connection with God. Remember my story about Wes, the young man who succeeded me as youth pastor at the first church I served? He was kind of a smart aleck, living on the edge, and not really caring about much of anything. Then I asked him to preside over the offering at our youth event and even say a prayer asking God to bless it. That's when God grabbed hold of Wes and changed his life, and I know that prayer was a big part of it. When Wes prayed, he suddenly knew for certain that Someone was listening—and that Someone was God! Wes had a calling into the ministry, but he didn't know it because he didn't know God.

Something similar happened in South America, where an atheist came up onstage with me to pray for a woman with an injured shoulder. As she prayed, she suddenly jumped back and began shaking her hands.

"My hands are tingling!" this atheist exclaimed.

God revealed to me at that moment that He was calling her into the healing ministry. He had a special anointing He wanted to give her, but she had spent her whole life turning away from Him. And, by the way, the other woman's injured shoulder was completely healed!

In New Jersey two years ago, I asked an atheist to pray for a man with a severely injured back. As he prayed, both men suddenly began to feel "heat and electricity" all over their bodies, and the man with the bad back was instantly healed. After the prayer, the atheist told me he would "have to reconsider" whether Jesus was real.

"How about if I pray that He will turn up the heat and electricity on you?" I asked. I did, and the Lord responded.

The young man, whom I'll call David, told me that he was blown away, although he was still not ready to make a public profession of faith in Christ. I was recently in the same city in New Jersey again to speak at the Vineyard church there, and David was present. He told me that he is now a passionate follower of Christ and shares his faith wherever he goes.

In Stavanger, Norway, I was helping lead a team out on the streets, when we wandered into a thrift store to look at some of the antiques. Inside, we met a woman who seemed to be in pain, so I asked her if she had pain in her hip.

"For many years," she said. She agreed that we could pray for her, and after we did, the pain completely left.

The woman's twenty-something daughter was with her, and I told her I sensed that Jesus wanted to heal her heart because of rejection she had experienced. Tears came to her eyes, and the team and I prayed for her as well.

During this time, another young woman was watching us out of the corner of her eye as she browsed through the shop. Finally, she spoke to us. "I'm sorry, but are you reading their aura or energy? How do you know these things?"

I said, "Oh no, this is by the power of the Holy Spirit that comes from being in a relationship with Jesus."

She nodded. "Oh. I'm an atheist, and I don't believe in Jesus."

I smiled and asked her, "Well, would you believe if you could feel Him or see Him?"

She shrugged and said, "That isn't possible!"

"Sure it is!" I said. "Put your hands out and close your eyes. I won't touch you, but you'll feel electricity, heat and heaviness from Jesus."

She did as I asked, and I asked Jesus to make Himself known to her. As she held her hands out, her eyelids began to flutter and her hands shook. When I asked her what she was feeling, she acknowledged heaviness and electricity in her hands.

When I asked the Lord to increase her sense of His presence, she gasped, her eyes popped open and her hands began trembling faster.

"I can't do this!" she said. "It's too strong!"

Looking straight into her eyes, I told her, "You just felt Jesus Christ and His power to save you."

Tears began to flow, and she said, "No! It has to be science!"

Before we left, I told her that the power of Jesus would come to her again that night, and she would have another opportunity to respond to Him and His salvation power.

"I don't know if I can handle it," she whispered.

"Just say yes to Jesus," I urged her, "because we can't handle life without Him."

A couple of months later, I received an email from someone in that city, telling me that the young woman had showed up at their church, told them about the encounter with God in the thrift store and said, "I have come here to accept Jesus, because I felt Him that day, though I didn't believe in Him."

I have seen so many miracles happen when atheists pray. You can read about more of those experiences in my two previous books, *Do What Jesus Did* and *Identity Thief.*

Go in Power

Sadly for me, and I hope for you, we have reached the end of our time together. But I hope we'll connect again soon. Please keep me informed as you go out to proclaim God's love and to show His mercy and power through signs and wonders. (You can find my contact information at the end of the book.)

Always remember that you don't have to do everything exactly right to get God to respond to you. Nor do you have to be perfect. He understands that we are fragile creatures who often make mistakes.

Too many people think they are not worthy of having God use them in a mighty way. Maybe you're one of them. But no matter what you think your shortcomings might be, you are wrong about yourself! God says you are capable of helping change the world, and He knows you better than you know yourself.

No matter what you've done or where you've been, never feel that God can't or won't use you. As you probably know, Charles Haddon Spurgeon was one of the great Christian leaders of the nineteenth century. Here's what he had to say to those who struggle to believe they are worthy of being used in God's service:

> You may be sighing and groaning because of inbred sin, and mourning over your darkness, yet the Lord sees "light" in your heart, for He has put it there, and all the cloudiness and gloom of your soul cannot conceal your light from His gracious eye. You may have sunk low in despondency, and even despair; but if your soul has any longing towards Christ, and if you

are seeking to rest in His finished work, God sees the "light." He not only sees, it, but He also preserves it in you. . . . The light thus preserved by His grace, He will one day develop into the splendor of noonday, and the fullness of glory. The light within is the dawn of the eternal day.[1]

Never forget that you have the light within you to *do greater things* for the Kingdom of God, *that the world may know Him.*

YOUR ACTIVATION GUIDE

- ► Why do you believe in Jesus? Think about how you would explain your faith to an atheist, as simply and as powerfully as possible.
- ► What are some of the reasons people struggle with their faith? What can we do, as believers, to help people overcome these barriers to belief?
- ► Have you ever struggled seriously with doubt? If so, what helped you put those doubts aside and learn to trust in Jesus?
- ► Do you believe that God hears and responds when atheists pray? Explain your answer.
- ► Do you have any friends who are atheists? If so, will you make a commitment to pray for them by name? What else can you do to reach them with Jesus' love?

NOTES

Chapter 1: An Army Is Rising Up

1. Will Reagan, "Break Every Chain," United Pursuit Music (Admin. by Capitol CMG Publishing), 2009.

2. Carol Wimber tells this story in more detail on the Vineyard's website, https://vineyardusa.org/library/how-the-vineyard-began.

3. Robby Dawkins, *Do What Jesus Did* (Minneapolis: Chosen Books, 2013), 36.

4. Ibid., 37.

Chapter 2: Greater Things across the World

1. John Wimber with Kevin Springer, *Power Evangelism* (New York: Harper & Row, 1986) 137.

2. R. Alan Woods, *John Wimber: Naturally Supernatural* (San Jacinto, Calif.: Rhema Rising Press, 2013), n.p.

3. For more information on Schools of Power and Love, visit http://powerandlove.org/team/tom-ruotolo/.

Chapter 3: Heal the Sick in the Name of Jesus

1. Joyce Meyer, as quoted at https://www.goodreads.com/quotes/389806-spending-time-with-god-is-the-key-to-our-strength.

Chapter 4: Speak His Words and Do His Works

1. Surprise Sithole, *Voice in the Night: The True Story of a Man and the Miracles That Are Changing Africa* (Minneapolis: Chosen Books, 2012), 15.

2. Dawkins, *Do What Jesus Did*, 112.

Chapter 6: Salvation Has Come

1. William J. Petersen and Randy Petersen, *100 Amazing Answers to Prayer* (Morgantown, Penn.: Masthof Press, 2015), 129–30.

Chapter 7: Vanquish Demons

1. C. S. Lewis, *The Screwtape Letters* (New York: Macmillan, 1961), 3–4.

Chapter 9: What to Do When Little Luci Fights Back

1. Tom Phillips, "China on Course to Become 'World's Most Christian Nation' within 15 Years," *The Telegraph*, April 19, 2014, http://www.telegraph .co.uk/news/worldnews/asia/china/10776023/China-on-course-to-become -worlds-most-Christian-nation-within-15-years.html.

2. For more on this, see Zhang Rongliang and Eugene Bach, *I Stand with Christ: The Courageous Life of a Chinese Christian* (New Kensington, Penn.: Whitaker House, 2015).

3. Rongliang and Bach, *I Stand With Christ*, 66–67.

4. Ibid., 68.

5. Brother Yun with Paul Hattaway, *The Heavenly Man: The Remarkable True Story of Chinese Christian Brother Yun* (Grand Rapids, Mich.: Kregel Books, 2002), 116–17.

6. Ibid., 193.

7. Ibid., 193.

8. Dr. William B. Salt, "How Does Resistance Training Build Muscle?" Sharecare, Inc., https://www.sharecare.com/health/resistance-training /how-resistance-training-build-muscle.

Chapter 11: Gaining the Victory in Jesus

1. "Entertainment: Highs and Lows," LVRJ.com, August 28, 2009, https:// www.reviewjournal.com/entertainment/highs-and-lows/.

2. Jennifer E. Jones, "Korn Meets Christ: The Conversion of Brian Welch," CBN.com, http://www1.cbn.com/korn-meets-christ-conversion -brian-welch-0.

3. "Brian Welch," Revolvy.com, https://www.revolvy.com/main/index .php?s=Brian%20Welch.

4. Jones, "Korn Meets Christ."

5. *Wikipedia*, s.v. "Charles Studd," last modified May 22, 2017, https:// en.wikipedia.org/wiki/Charles_Studd.

Chapter 12: Amazing Things Happen When Atheists Pray

1. Charles Haddon Spurgeon, *Morning & Evening* (Ross-Shire, Scotland; Christian Focus Publications, 1994), 19.

Robby Dawkins and his wife, Angie, have been married 25 years and have six sons, one daughter-in-law, one grandson and a beloved dog named Bear. Robby is a fifth-generation pastor born to a missionary family in Japan. He served as a youth pastor for twelve years before planting a Vineyard church in Aurora, Illinois, where 70 percent of members came to Christ at the church and 60 percent were saved through power encounters. In 2013, the mayor of Aurora, along with the chief of police, bestowed upon Robby and his church an acknowledgment that they had made a significant difference in Aurora's crime-rate reduction. Robby and Angie served the Aurora church from 1996 to 2013.

Today, Robby travels extensively as an itinerant minister, crossing denominational and nondenominational lines to equip churches in power ministry. He has spoken in 51 countries, including some on the Voice of the Martyrs organization's most dangerous countries in the world list. He has addressed audiences of more than fifteen thousand people. Robby has been featured in the movies *Furious Love* (2010), *Father of Lights* (2012), *Holy Ghost: Reborn* (2015) and *Finger of God 2* (2018), and he will appear in several other upcoming documentaries. He also has appeared on God TV, TBN UK, TBN US and Sid Roth's *It's Supernatural!* His book *Do What Jesus Did* (2013) ranked on three of Amazon's bestseller lists and met with success in the United States, the United Kingdom and Europe. His book *Identity Thief* (2015) gained similar applause and attention.

For more information, visit www.robbydawkins.com. Connect with Robby on Facebook www.facebook.com/robbydawkins ministries or on Twitter www.twitter.com/robbydawkins.